THE PATTERN OF THE PAST:

Can We Determine It?

The Pattern of the Past:

CAN WE DETERMINE IT?

BY

PIETER GEYL

ARNOLD J. TOYNBEE

AND

PITIRIM A. SOROKIN

Boston · THE BEACON PRESS · *1949*

Contents

THE PATTERN OF THE PAST:

Can We Determine It?

Toynbee's System of Civilizations

By PIETER GEYL

1

To SURVEY HISTORY AS A WHOLE, to discover trends in its movement, to seek out its meaning—Professor Toynbee is not the first to undertake the attempt. He joins the company of St. Augustine and Bossuet, Voltaire, Hegel, Marx, Buckle, Wells, Spengler; nor is he the least among them.

Six volumes now lie before us, three published in 1934, three in 1939 [*A Study of History;* Oxford University Press]; and that another three will complete the work may well turn out to be an illusion. What we have so far been given is an imposing achievement. The reading, the learning, are almost without precedent. Toynbee moves confidently in the histories of the old civilizations of Asia, the Chinese and the Indian, of Egypt, of America as well. He is thoroughly acquainted with Roman and especially with Hellenic history. Classical literature he also knows, and when I say knows, I mean he is profoundly familiar with it and is able to draw on it freely to evoke a deeper background for his arguments and his reflections. And indeed for that purpose he has a great deal more at his disposal, above all, the Bible. Toynbee lives with the Bible, and its texts lie scattered thickly over his pages. But from Goethe too, from Shakespeare and from Marvell, from Shelley, Blake, Meredith, he quotes liberally. He knows how to use for his arguments modern ethnological, sociological, philosophical, psychological concepts. At the same time he himself writes in a splendid, full and supple style, which retains command over this wealth of quotations by a constant flow of images and with an intense and untiring vividness of argument. And, what is still more important, this rich and variegated abundance serves a majestic vision. He is sensitive to the colorful world of phenomena, to life; but above all he is profoundly aware of the unity of the architectural pattern into which he fits—a remarkable mind, unusual in our every-day world of historians.

In his first volume, that is, in 1934, Professor Toynbee announced thirteen parts to be treated successively in his work. Of these, with the appearance of Volume VI, five have been dealt with; the remaining eight will, he expects, demand less space. What a plan! What especially fills one with awe is to

see the author from his first volume onward referring
to later parts which are to appear after an unknown
number of years and of volumes. As he proceeds,
there are cross-references backwards and forwards.
In his mind evidently the immense structure forms a
unity.

His work is intended to be a comparative study of
civilizations as a basis for general conceptions about
history. Civilizations are for him the real units of
history, not states, which he is wont to indicate con-
temptuously as "parochial," or nations, whose hyper-
trophied self-consciousness, under the description
"nationalism," he detests.

In the six thousand years of which we have knowledge, he lists twenty-one such civilizations. He enu-
merates them, fixes their mutual relationships—in so
far as they were not self-contained, which is a rare
occurrence—and observes that they are all decayed
or have perished, with the exception of Western
civilization, that is the Latin-Christian civilization,
which he represents as having sprung from the Hellenic, in its Roman phase. About the prospects of
this, our own civilization, that big swallow-all, Professor Toynbee leaves us in uncertainty; he has already repeatedly touched upon the problem, but only
in his twelfth part will he treat it thoroughly. Mean-
while he believes it possible, even at this stage in his

investigation, to state rules; sometimes he uses the word *laws*, on other occasions he speaks of *standard patterns of development*, of *tendencies* occurring in certain circumstances.

How do civilizations *come into being?* Not by climate, soil, or situation favoring the process; on the contrary, by overcoming obstacles: thus the shock is administered by which portions of mankind have passed out of the equilibrium of an existence without, or before, civilization, "from the integration of custom to the differentiation of civilization." The author proceeds to examine these adverse conditions at length under a number of headings: "hard countries," "blows," "pressures," "penalizations." "Challenge and response" is the formula in which he summarizes this movement in human history, a rhythm which makes itself felt over the entire field of human action.

Next comes the *growth* of civilizations. There is an increasing command over the environment, in the first place the physical environment; there follows a process of what Toynbee terms "etherealization," in which the physical environment loses its importance, and action shifts from outside to within. Progressive differentiation is and remains typical of the process of growth. Here too we are shown in all stages the action of challenge and response. But the author thinks it possible to be more specific: the growth of a civilization takes place through creative persons or creative minorities, whose action is conditioned by a movement of "withdrawal and return." The larger half of Volume III is taken up by illustrations of this process.

In Volume IV the phenomenon of the *breakdown* of civilization is discussed. The vast majority of civilizations known to us have after a longer or a shorter period been overtaken by this fate. The duration of growth differs greatly. It is not possible therefore to speak of a normal stretch of time from rise to breakdown, and Toynbee expressly denies that the decline is inherent in an iron law of fate such as governs the physical world. The decay proceeds from the doomed civilization itself, but it must be understood as the result of a shortcoming not decreed by any law; it is a human failure, there is no necessity about it.

The volume is mainly devoted to an analysis of the causes of breakdown. Very emphatically he rejects the view that the downfall can be ascribed to forces from the outside. He finds the causes of breakdown in the retarding force which arises from the mechanical element in the "mimesis" of the majority—that very mimesis through which the creative personality or minority can obtain a hold on them; in the

"intractability of institutions," giving them a paralyz-
ing or vitiating effect (he mentions very dissimilar instances, like those of democracy and industrialism
acting upon "parochial" sovereignty, the effect of
"parochialism" on churches, of religion on caste systems); in what he calls "the nemesis of creativity," the
stiffening or exhaustion following upon creative action, as exemplified in the "idolization" of an achievement or of an attainment, of an institution, of a technique; under this heading he brings the intoxication
of successful violence, militarism, triumph—not only
in the military sense, though, for of the historical examples with which he illustrates his argument, none
is elaborated at greater length than that of the
papacy, which, after having been carried by Gregory
VII to the height of power, was ruined by the blind
self-conceit of Boniface VIII. (This, by the way, is
his method throughout: a large number of particular
cases, from antiquity or from modern times, from
alien and distant civilizations and from our own, is
always adduced to prove the theses presented.)

Breakdown is followed by *disintegration*. This
process is studied in Volumes V and VI. Nowhere
else in human history has Professor Toynbee found
so fixed a regularity. The "creative minority" changes
into a "ruling minority," the masses into a "prole-

tariat"—a word by which Toynbee, detaching it from its now usual narrower meaning, understands a group which has no longer any real share in the civilization of its society. This is the "schism," for him the first sign of a civilization's having broken down— a schism into three parts, for besides the ruling minority there emerges "an internal and an external proletariat," which latter clashes against the frontiers of the State or the Empire of the ruling minority. The course of history proceeds by the rhythm of challenge and response; but while a growing society has always been able to find the right answer, and is therefore faced each time by a different challenge, a broken-down society can no longer really succeed; it is at best able to put off the evil day and finds itself after some time confronted again by the same problem. In the souls of men, too, the schism can be observed. Social disharmony creates a feeling of impotence, of sin; the standards of style and of behavior get out of order; ways out of the unbearable present are tried through "archaism"— back to the past, or through "futurism"—a leap into the future; or an attempt is made to detach oneself from society by means of philosophy or of religion. Toynbee here discerns the working of another form of challenge and response, "schism and palingenesis":

a higher religion is founded by the proletariat segregating itself from society, although the creation is only apparently due to the majority. The external proletariat reacts through the formation of "war bands" and "heroic poetry." In any case this movement does not touch the now doomed society. Its history is governed by another variant of the rhythm, "rout and rally." The rout takes the form of ever more violent wars between states conscious only of their independence; this is "the Time of Troubles," another sign of a broken-down civilization. The rally materializes in a "universal state," the best creative work of which a ruling minority is capable. But the breathing-space of the *pax oecumenica* is of short duration, the universal state brings in its train only an "Indian summer," soon it is troubled again—another rout, followed by another rally, until the rout, each time worse than before, can no longer be stayed and leads to dissolution, to ruin. This is not, of course, the end of all things. A new civilization has been preparing itself, chrysalis-like woven into the Universal Church, a creation of the Schismatic Proletariat, and this now unfolds itself.

As for the action of individuals in these circumstances, however brightly the creative spark may glow within them, it is doomed to failure. Professor Toynbee distinguishes four kinds of Saviors of Society—for this is the shape in which the great man now appears: by the sword, by power; by an appeal to the past or to the future—these two are the attempts to save society itself; then there are the two kinds of those who want to save man *from* society: the founders of a philosophy who, however, work only for the ruling minority, and the founders of a religion, whose empire is not of this world.

Professor Toynbee believes he has observed in history that this decline of a civilization after its break down follows a much more regular course than the growing process, to which no inescapable limit has been set. He has been so much struck by the uniformity with which the various "institutions" and phases—Time of Troubles, Universal State, Indian Summer, Universal Church, External War Bands and Heroic Age—spring from the body of a disintegrating civilization that he has reduced it all to a table.[1] Stronger still is the similarity of the psychological condition of men in disintegrating civilizations. The general tendency can be characterized by the word "standardization": the result of all this violent movement is therefore exactly the reverse of that in growing civilizations, where it leads to differentiation. And it develops, in rout and rally, sub-rout and sub-rally, down to catastrophe, in three and a half beats.

[1] See footnote 21 below.

2

Here we have the dry bones of a system to which the author gives flesh and life. The idea inspiring him is that of Christianity. It is true that Toynbee at times recalls Spengler, and his view of history is in fact not unrelated to the *Untergang des Abendlandes*. He expressly rejects Spengler's identification of civilizations with animate beings, which are born, are young, grow older, and die; when they break down it is by their own act alone. Similarly, he speaks emphatically against Spengler's connecting civilization with race. But if he insists on the freedom of choice, on the spiritual factor unrelated to blood or to the perishable flesh, he too carries to great lengths the presentation of his civilizations as well-rounded units. Above all, during the centuries-long process of disintegration following upon breakdown, he sees them subjected to a regularity of decay hardly less rigid than Spengler's parallel with the biological process.

In any case, however much he may diverge from Spengler, his system is even more diametrically opposed to historical materialism. He may speak of laws, his mind may be stocked richly with scientific notions, from which his language is ever borrowing terms and images; in reality the sovereignty and the

freedom of the spirit are his main concern, and his
Bible texts are more than a mere decoration of his
argument, for in them he finds his profoundest truths
foreshadowed and confirmed. God become man in
Christ is to him the veritable sense of history. Of the
great constructors of systems, St. Augustine is most
closely related to him in spirit, and Professor Toynbee himself, in the preface to his second series, written in that gloomy year 1939, brings respectful
homage to the bishop who completed *De Civitate
Dei* while the Vandals were besieging his episcopal
town. Material advantage is nothing in Toynbee's
view; it is obstacles which rouse the spirit to consciousness. Violence he detests, he is a searcher after
"gentleness." He meets history with ethical apprecia-
tions. The spirit, the highly gifted individual, the
small group, these are the sources of creative force.
Power is an illusion, if not a boomerang. As a
civilization grows, it etherealizes. What exactly does
he mean by this? He expresses it in morphological, in
biological, in philosophical, and finally also in religious terms. No doubt all the rest for him is com-
prehended in the phrase belonging to the last-named
category, according to which etherealization means:
" a conversion of the soul from the World, the Flesh,
and the Devil, to the Kingdom of Heaven." [2]

[2] III, 192.

But of what use to us is his system? To what extent does it clear up our insight into history, help us in disentangling its mysteries, contain the solutions which, each in our own particularist or parochial sphere, we have so far looked for in vain? A system which is presented to us, not as springing from the author's mind or imagination or faith, but as carefully built up in the course of empirical research—for this, we are told all through the voluminous work, is its method: we are the spectators of an expedition in quest of the norms, the regularity, the laws, of the historical process, and before our eyes the traveler gathers his data, from which, so he maintains, each time assuming our assent, his conclusions impose themselves, a system thus presented ought to render to all of us these very services. But to me at least it does not do so. Splendid as the qualities of the work are, fascinating as I have found it, grateful as I shall ever remain to the author for profound remarks, striking parallels, wide prospects, and other concomitant beauties—the system seems to me useless.

My most essential criticism, the criticism which embraces all others, is connected with this claim that his whole argument is based on empirical methods, in which it seems to me the author is deceiving himself. Had he really examined history with an open mind, merely formulating the theses supplied him by the observed facts, phenomena, developments, he could never have printed that imposing announcement of the division into so many parts in the opening pages of his first volume, nor could he in his references, as early as 1934, indicate what he was going to say about various chief problems in part 9 or in part 13, in 1950 or in 1960. Not that this is the ground of my doubting the genuineness of his empirical method; that is to be found in my examination of the six volumes themselves. The learning is miraculous, the wealth of examples and parallels overwhelming. But alas! the wealth of human history is ever so much greater. On looking closely, after having rubbed his dazzled eyes, the reader will see that Toynbee does not after all serve up more than a tiny spoonful out of the great cauldron. But no! this is a misleading comparison. When you fish in a cauldron you cannot select, and to select is exactly what he is doing all the time: he selects the instances which will support his theses, or he presents them in the way that suits him, and he does so with an assurance which hardly leaves room for the suspicion, not only that one might quote innumerable others with which his theses would not bear company, but especially that those cases he does mention can be explained or described in a different way so as to disagree no less completely with his theses.

3

So to me the rules, the laws, the standard patterns, laid down by the author after he has expounded examples and arguments at length and with never-failing gusto, do not seem to possess more than a very limited validity. At times they are no more than truisms. In any case, all these formulas of regularity, these distinctions alleged to present themselves in a fixed order, and these schemes of parallel development do not seem to be of much practical use. Personally, at least, I do not know how to work with them, let alone (and this, strictly speaking, ought to be possible) to make them operate unerringly.

Take even the striking formula of challenge and response. This—or its application from the science of psychology to history—must be pronounced a find. It hits off happily a form of movement in human communal life. There is no question here of a law, there is merely an observation of a frequent occurrence. But it will deepen our insight when in coming across a case of this description, we are conscious of its belonging to one of the usual categories of life. However, Professor Toynbee cannot stop there. He thinks he can state as a general rule that the easier the environment the less is the incitement to civilization man finds in it. And indeed one can hardly imagine the Land of Cockaigne becoming the cradle of so active a thing as a civilization. But now this lover of systems begins to ask whether perhaps the stimulus to civilization becomes stronger as the environment is more arduous. He therefore applies "our now well-tried empirical method" [3] and in fact is able to adduce a number of striking instances. Art and labor had to be expended in making the valley of the Yellow River habitable, and even then it remained exposed to devastating floods; in that of the Yangtse, where the soil is equally fertile, no such terrible inconvenience is to be feared; and yet Chinese civilization came to birth not on the Yangtse but on the Yellow River. There is also the well-known contrast between the fat land of Boeotia and stony Attica—and everybody knows to which of the two Hellenic civilization owes the greater debt. Twelve more such cases are expounded, and later, after having shown by a number of instances how blows, pressures and penalizations evoke similar reactions, Toynbee writes that one might incline to the view that " 'the greater the challenge, the greater the stimulus' is a law which knows no limits to its validity. We have not stumbled upon any palpable limits at any point in our empirical survey so far." [4]

[3] II, 31.   [4] II, 260.

To my ears this has a rather naive sound. But just as I am on the point of arguing that fourteen cases of "hard countries," and perhaps a few dozen of each of the other kinds of obstacles, do not really amount to very much, and that it is hardly permissible to speak of empiricism unless the readers can test this so-called "law" by the hundreds or thousands of other cases they can dig up out of history—the author surprises me by announcing with an air of triumph that under the heading of "hard countries" he has not even mentioned two of the most striking examples, Venice and Holland. "What challenge could be more extreme than the challenge presented by the sea to Holland and to Venice? What more extreme, again, than the challenge presented by the Alps to Switzerland? And what responses could be more magnificent than those which Holland, Venice, and Switzerland have made? The three hardest pieces of country in Western Europe have stimulated their inhabitants to attain the highest level of social achievement that has yet been attained by any of the peoples of Western Christendom."

"Oh land wrung from the waves!" Every Dutchman has heard innumerable times his people's sterling qualities explained from their age-long struggle with the water. And nobody will contest that here is one factor in the building up of our special

type of society. He who has kept hold of the thread
of Toynbee's argument, however, will reflect that
our author is really engaged in a discussion of the
origins of civilizations, and of civilizations in the
sense in which he calls them pre-eminently "fields
of historical study," those twenty-one civilizations of
his. The civilization of Holland, however, is no more
than a parochial part of the great Western civilization. Of the *originating* of a civilization in the hard
conditions of the Dutch soil there can therefore be
no question. I note in passing that Professor Toynbee repeatedly commits this error—an error against
his own method. But even if we overlooked this and
permitted him to adduce *national* instances, we
would still have to remark that even within the Netherlands community the form peculiar to Holland
(the Western seaboard province of which Toynbee
is obviously thinking) cannot be regarded as original. If one looks a little more closely, one will observe that within the European and even within the
Netherlands cultural area the rise of Holland was
fairly late, and this no doubt as a result of these very
conditions created by sea and rivers. If in the end
it overcame these conditions, it was not without the
assistance of the surrounding higher forms of civilization (even the Romans and their dyke-building had
an important share in making the region habitable).

But can even after that initial stage the continued struggle with the water be decisive in explaining the later prosperity and cultural fecundity of the country? Is it not indispensable to mention the excellence of the soil, once it had become possible to make use of it? and above all the situation, which promoted the rise of shipping and of a large international commerce? Was the case of Holland then wholly due to hard conditions after all? Is it right to isolate that factor from among the multifarious complexity of reality and to suppress the favoring factors? And, we cannot refrain from wondering, would it not be necessary to apply a similar argument to the majority of Professor Toynbee's few dozen cases?

It would carry me too far if I attempted this.[5] It is well-known that demonstrating an error demands more time than committing it. Let me merely

[5] I draw attention to what in II, 108, is said about the respective positions of France, Germany and England at the moment when that volume was written (1931). Perhaps it is unfair to pick on that passage, because the fifteen years which have since elapsed supply us with so convenient a standard of criticism; here is at least proof how little guarantee of objectivity there is in Toynbee's so-called empirical method.—Take II, 70, where the New Englanders' success in the struggle for the North American continent with their Spanish, Dutch, French and Southern rivals is said to throw light on the question of the different degrees of hardness in the physical environment of human existence and their stimulating effect. As if the assistance given or not given by the various mother countries had not been really decisive, not to speak of various other factors! But there would be no end if one went on to discuss particular cases.

make this general remark, that each of the instances discussed by Professor Toynbee of "blows" which had an invigorating effect is necessarily related by him in an extremely simplified form. But in the presentation of history simplification means, if not falsification, at least emphasizing one particular side of a matter which in reality had an infinite number of facets. Every historical fact—he himself mentions the objection he knows very well will be raised against his method—is unique and therefore incomparable with other historical facts. His reply is that the facts, in some respects unique, and in so far incomparable, belong in other respects to a class and are in so far comparable. There is truth in this—else no general ideas about history could ever be formulated—, but isolating the comparable elements is ticklish work. In a certain sense no historical fact is detachable from its circumstances, and by eliminating the latter violence is done to history. There is hardly an incident or a phenomenon quoted by Toynbee to illustrate a particular thesis which does not give rise to qualifications in the reader's mind—if the reader is conversant with the matter! Most of the time our author is writing about Greek or Arabic or Hittite or Cretan or Japanese history, where one—where I at least—find it more difficult to check him.

Professor Toynbee himself, however, feels that he

cannot raise the intensity of his "challenges" indefinitely. It is in fact very simple, one does not need
to conduct a learned, allegedly empirical, historical
investigation. If I give you a blow on the head it is
very likely that your energy will be strongly roused
and that you will strike back with vigor; but the
blow may prove so powerful that you will not have
anything to reply, that (to put it in the style of Toynbee) the source of your energy will dry up for ever.
In the world of communities it is likely enough that
things will pass off in a similar fashion. So we see
Professor Toynbee soon meditating "an over-riding
law to the effect that 'the most stimulating challenge is to be found in a mean between a deficiency
of severity and an excess of it,'" after which we get
another 130 pages or more—under a chapter heading
"The Golden Mean"—with instances of succumbing
under pressure all too heavy or blows all too hard.
One cannot refrain from the liveliest admiration for
the rich variety of his knowledge, for the ease with
which, after having sounded the causes of the downfall of Irish civilization, he does the same for the
Icelandic, only to proceed with unflagging vivacity
to Arabic history; until at long last he ventures to
conclude: "There are challenges of a salutary severity that stimulate the human subject of the ordeal
to a creative response; but there are also challenges

of an overwhelming severity to which the human subject succumbs." My observation with regard to the blow on your head has a less impressive sound, but does it not convey precisely the same meaning? Yet our author is not yet satisfied. He repeats the phrase coined at the outset of his argument, "a mean between a deficiency of severity and an excess of it," and this time introduces it with the magic words: "In scientific terminology. . . ."

So here we have a "law," scientifically established, or at least scientifically formulated. But what next? When we try to apply it, we shall first of all discover that in every given historical situation it refers to only one element, one out of many, one which, when we are concerned with historical presentation, cannot be abstracted from the others. Moreover, is it not essential to define what is too much and what too little, to stipulate where the golden mean lies? As to that, the "law" has nothing to say. That has to be defined anew each time by observation.

4

Before Professor Toynbee sets out in his third volume to treat the problem of the growth of civilizations, he disposes of the arrested civilizations known to history. These constitute a heterogeneous group: the Polynesians, the Eskimos, the Nomads, the Os-

manlis and the Spartans. The general explanation
is that in these cases the challenge was so serious—
a challenge of nature in the first three, of the need
of keeping large subject populations under control
in the latter two—as to impose a system of defense
which through its demands or its artificiality used up
all energies; an equilibrium was thus brought about,
from which there was no getting away. One is struck
by the immense ingenuity. The circumstances are in
each of the five cases related not only vividly, but
with a subtle sense of distinctions. Yet all this hardly
makes it convincing. The heterogeneousness alone
—Eskimos and Turks!—raises doubts in the mind. As
far as the Eskimos are concerned, the explanation
adduced is certainly plausible. But in the case of the
Turks? That slave court, that peculiar method of
fighting and governing by means of a special class,
and slaves at that! and kidnapped boys of alien
origin!—here is indeed a system we can well imagine
did not allow of cultural development. But why
should it arrest the civilization indefinitely? Why
was it not possible to get away from it, or, when it
was got rid of, why did not something better take
its place? In the case of the Eskimos, struggling
with the unchanging conditions of the Polar sea,
this immutability is not surprising, but in the other
case it is, and so a formula intended to cover both

cases does not help much. Let us take another example of our own. Take the German Order in the
Baltic lands. Here too we have a most artificial institution, built for fighting and for ruling. Yet here the
populations were Christianized and Germanized, and
with the dissolution of the Knightly Order merged
into the great German civilization.

The usefulness of these general explanations, of
this tabularizing, is not very apparent. Within the
subdivisions the similarity is not only vague, but at
times forced, and we feel that it is just the differences
which matter.

Extremely dubious also, it seems to me, is the
withdrawal-and-return theory, with which the re-
mainder of this volume is taken up. This is the movement by which personalities and minorities prepare
themselves for their creative task in a growing civilization. Even at first glance we wonder what the
author will be able to make of the twenty-six or
twenty-seven personalities he has selected as examples—men of all times and of all lands, princes and
statesmen, saints, historians. What, we ask, can be
the connecting element between Peter the Great
and Émile Ollivier (and was the latter a great personality?), between St. Paul, Machiavelli, the Bud-
dha and Dante? A more careful reading only
strengthens the impression. This chapter is hardly

an example of valid method. In some cases Professor Toynbee gives complete life histories, full of particulars which have nothing to do with the point at issue; in others he is very brief. The difference in treatment seems wholly arbitrary. But even the point all his heroes have in common, that they withdrew and after a while returned, is governed by arbitrariness. The withdrawal of one was compulsory, of another voluntary. Peter the Great set out to travel in order to learn and came back in order to put into practice his newly acquired knowledge and to rule; Émile Ollivier had to expatriate himself after 1870, remained outside politics for the rest of his life, never was able to free his mind from the tragedy of the Second Empire, and in his old age, having long before returned to France, wrote a book in many volumes about it. Professor Toynbee also mentions Kant and in a few lines describes the philosopher living quietly at Koenigsberg while his thought radiated over the world. But how precisely did he "return"? In this way one can include anybody to whom one takes a fancy. Not that it would not be easy to add more typical cases to the list: there is William the Silent (1567–72), Napoleon (Egypt), Luther (the Wartburg), Guido Gezelle, the Flemish poet (the exile at Bruges and at Courtrai)—but why continue the search? It cannot on the other hand be maintained—nor does Professor Toynbee try—that in all great lives there occurs such a period of interruption. I should not know how to include either Raphael or Vondel in the list, nor most of the great princely rulers: neither Louis XIV nor Saint Louis, neither Philip the Good nor Charles V. Is it that in these cases the rule is suspended by the peculiar conditions attached to hereditary leadership? But De Witt, too, never paused to take breath, and when he withdrew it was not to return. Nor did Shakespeare: the one was murdered, the other spent his last years peacefully as a landed gentleman. What law can we discern in all this?

Things do not improve when minorities are discussed. Professor Toynbee first mentions some penalized minorities, to observe how they acquire particular strength in their retirement and arm for their return to play important parts. Thus for instance the English Nonconformists, who after having their share in the commotions of the middle of the seventeenth century withdrew—rather, were excluded from everything!—withdrew into the world of business to return omnipotent and to become the authors of the Industrial Revolution. No doubt, there is something in this. In Dutch history, too, the Baptists towards the close of the Republican period, during which they had been kept out of the govern-

ment, were among the greatest capitalists. One is at
first inclined to point to the Dutch Catholics as forming an objection to the theory. Here you have a group
who had also been compelled to throw themselves
into non-political activities, but who even after their
emancipation were not able to play more than a
fairly modest part in economic life. One reflects,
however, that the ever-growing power of the Catholics in present-day political life in Holland might
well be connected with their exclusion in the past,
for that is what taught them to prize their cohesion
and organization. But other doubts are already as-
sailing the reader's mind. Is not that peculiarity inherent in the spirit of Catholicism? Of modern
Catholicism at least, and one thinks of Trent: is not
this militancy of modern Catholicism the response to
the challenge of the Reformation? The Toynbee
terminology comes to mind very readily. But it never
gets one very far. The differences will not be denied.
Here comparable developments go faster, there more
slowly, here they are stronger, there weaker, or they
take this direction and elsewhere another direction. And the exceptions! Professor Toynbee mentions the English Nonconformists. Why does he not
mention the English Catholics? These, when they
"returned" after their long exclusion, were certainly
not "omnipotent"!

But Professor Toynbee now attempts to bring certain decisive developments in Hellenic and in Western history within the scope of this same motive. In his view—and he is not the first to make the observation—there is a similarity between Athens, which made herself "the education of Hellas," and Italy, which filled the same part with respect to Western Europe. When he pictures Athens withdrawing from the eighth to the sixth century B.C., and Italy from the thirteenth to the fifteenth centu~ /, and argues that in each case this minority i~ ᐧ retirement devoted th~ ᵧₑ releaased by relinquishing its share in foreign entanglements to the task of solving the problem facing the whole of its society (that is, of Hellas and of Western Europe respectively) by an original solution of its own, the construction strikes me as hopelessly far-fetched. And indeed the whole of Western European history (to confine myself to that) has to be bent askew so as to allow the thesis to be carried through. The thesis is, that in Ital~ there was developed the modern State, albeit on the city plan only, which became for Western Europe the model in its struggle to free itself from feudalism. True, there were city-states on this side of the Alps, in Germany, in Flanders: as early as the middle of the fourteenth century "the feudal darkness of the Western world was thickly sown with constellations

of city-states." [6] In fact Professor Toynbee here sees
the same motive in action: "a creative minority ex-
tricated itself from the general political life of the
Western Society by building city walls and learning
to live a new life of its own behind them." Italy, however, was a decisive factor, and this we are to view
as the return of Italy. Is it not evident that a development proper to Western Europe herself was at
least as important, and that Italy, moreover, did not
so much return as was sought out in her seclusion?

But the train of thought is continued, this time
with Holland, Switzerland, and more particularly
England as the protagonists. In the new chapter of
European history opened in the sixteenth century the
problem was: how can the entire Western world take
over, albeit on the scale of kingdom-states, this new
Italian and Flemish way of life? "This challenge was
taken up in Switzerland, Holland, and England, and
it received eventually an English answer." [7] We are
here given, it must be said, a very peculiar and personal and certainly most incomplete view of European history in the post-mediaeval period, and that it
should be necessary to begin this way in order to
bring in the withdrawal-and-return motive hardly inspires confidence. And how is it introduced into the
picture this time? Holland behind her dykes, Switzer-

[6] III, 346.   [7] III, 351.

land in her Alps, England behind the Channel, were able to stand aside and thus to prepare their contribution. In the cases of Holland and of Switzerland, our author continues, the safeguards proved in the long run ineffective. (I state in passing, without laboring the point, that in the case of Holland at least, at a time when Amsterdam was the great international banking center, Dutch merchant fleets covered all the seas, Dutch diplomacy was active and Dutch intellectual life giving and taking incessantly, there was not the slightest question of seclusion; while neither of the two countries can justly be described as a very striking instance of a free state which had at the same time solved the problem of modern state organization!)

But now we are left with England alone. That the peculiar English form of government, which in the nineteenth century was to exercise so wide an influence, owes something of its development to England's relatively safe situation, is a current and indeed altogether acceptable view. But there are of course a good many more factors to be taken into account, and the picture of a creative minority in quiet and retirement devoting itself to that problem strikes one as somewhat overdrawn. Professor Toynbee, however, is still not satisfied and starts systematizing in a really dizzy fashion.

It is true, he argues, that it was against their own inclination that the English were released from their entanglement in the affairs of the continent. (He places the event between 1429, when the death of Henry V and the intervention of Jeanne d'Arc brought about a turn in the Hundred Years War,[8] and in 1558, when Bloody Mary lost Calais.) But subsequently they came to realize that this had been "a blessing in disguise" and fought as hard to save themselves from new entanglements as they had once done to keep them: see their resistance to the successive attempts of Philip II, of Louis XIV, and of Napoleon to fit England into a continental European empire. (An untenable simplification of at least Louis XIV's intentions; but let this pass.)

Might it not be said with equal justice that the English in that second series of wars, besides being moved by the most natural of all instincts, that of self-preservation, were still striving, though in another way, after power outside their island? Were not the true isolationists in England—and there were such, in the sixteenth, in the seventeenth and in the eighteenth centuries—intent on keeping out of those wars? And was the loss of positions on the continent

[8] III, 366. According to G. M. Trevelyan as well, *History of England*, these two events "saved the British Constitution." A curious way of putting it: in those times the *British* constitution still lay hidden in the womb of the future.

really recognized as a blessing in disguise? Yes, in so far as the view gradually gained ground that dominion over part of France was an illusion. Yet Cromwell got hold of Dunkirk, and a generation or more afterwards England seized Gibraltar, which she was never to let go. Malta, moreover, may not be situated on the continent, but the clue to England's possession of that island is hardly to be found in her anxiety to live in seclusion.

Professor Toynbee goes on imperturbably building up his system. These periods of relative isolation (which in England, according to him, began with the loss of Calais, with the accession of Elizabeth) generally fall into two phases. "The first, or originative phase is a youthful age of poetry and romance and emotional upheaval and intellectual ferment; the second, or constructive phase is a comparatively sedate and 'grown-up' age of prose and matter-of-fact and common sense and systematization." For Italy he exemplifies the two phases in Dante and Boccaccio respectively (although Dante was certainly not lacking in systematizing capacity and his high poetry is as far removed from youthful emotion or romanticism as from common sense and matter-of-factness!). In Athens he discerns the dividing point in the disaster of 404 B.C. (when, it seems to me, the time to speak of isolation was long past). In England, finally, the first phase runs from Elizabeth down to the Restoration of 1660, and the second from then on to about 1860 or 1870.

One imagines that the characterization of the two phases was primarily inspired by English cultural history (not that Shakespeare or Milton, the latter expressly mentioned by Professor Toynbee, can really be lumped together in the description "youthful romanticism"). The constructive phase of England's creative isolation, at any rate, to let Professor Toynbee put it in his own words, has "to its credit such solid achievements as the foundation of the Royal Society and 'the Glorious Revolution of 1688' and the peopling of the North American Continent with an English-speaking population and *The History of the Decline and Fall of the Roman Empire* and the invention of the steam-engine and the passage of the Reform Bill of 1832 and the establishment of the Indian Empire and *The Origin of Species* (which was published in 1859) and the invention of the British Commonwealth of self-governing nations (an invention which dates from the creation of the Dominion of Canada in 1867)."

What is one to say of such a passage in this brilliant work? Does England really owe all these heterogeneous achievements to her isolation? England, Professor Toynbee writes, was dragged back into con-

tinental European entanglements by the war of 1914.
I have already remarked that the wars against Philip
II, against Louis XIV, against Napoleon, were just
as much evidence of England's uninterrupted community with the rest of Europe. The whole of this
suggestion of an isolation lasting from 1558 to 1914,
or at least to 1870, is completely untenable. The
Glorious Revolution is indeed a fine example of the
great deeds which England was able to achieve
through her seclusion! Have William the Third and
his Dutchmen been forgotten? Professor Toynbee
seems here to have strayed into an extreme insularity
such as Macaulay could not have improved upon: one
would have thought this had become impossible
since Ranke. And now take cultural life. How deeply
imbued with Italian influences were Shakespeare and
his contemporaries! How strong were the spiritual
ties connecting the Puritans, and Milton, with the
Reformed confessions on the continent! Was not
French influence a dominating force after 1660? and,
inversely, how directly did English influence make
itself felt on French, and, generally speaking, on Continental thought in the eighteenth century! Toynbee mentions Gibbon; but can Gibbon be imagined
without French "philosophy"? Read Hammond's
Gladstone and the Irish Nation, and you will see
how intensely a great mid-nineteenth-century Eng-

lishman took part in European intellectual life.

One cannot help asking, furthermore, whether it really was only in the second half of the nineteenth century, or even in the twentieth, on England's "return," to use Professor Toynbee's expression, that England's contribution to Western civilization, allegedly prepared in isolation during that lengthy period, reached the rest of the world. I have hinted already how very far from true this was for the eighteenth century; but no less great and no less fruitful was the "Anglomania" in the first half of the nineteenth century. Yet another question presents itself, whether other nations, which had not withdrawn themselves, which throughout that period were in the thick of European entanglements (to follow for a moment this unacceptable thesis of England's aloofness), whether in particular France, did not by any chance make a creative contribution? The question is absurd. But all these pages of Toynbee's are fantastic.

5

We come to Volume IV, which deals with the breakdown of civilizations. Professor Toynbee begins with an attempt to prove that these breakdowns are not in general brought about by external forces. On looking closely we soon discover that the author does some violence to the facts to make them fit this

thesis. We have only to look at his list of sixteen de-
funct civilizations (sixteen out of the twenty-one, to
which are to be added five arrested and four abortive
ones) to think at once that it will be difficult in several cases to escape the verdict: death by external
violence.

Leaving aside the old Arabic and Hittite civilizations (about which more in a moment), this suspicion arises in connection with the old American
civilizations, that of the Incas, and the Mexican and
Yucatan (or Mayan); also with the Turkish (not the
only, but certainly the most striking, case of arrested
civilizations long ago broken down and now decayed)
and with the Scandinavian and old Irish (broken
down before birth and now dead). Professor Toynbee admits that the ruin of the Inca civilization is
often quoted as an example of ruin through external
interference. He proceeds to argue, however, that
the destruction by the Spaniards of the *empire* of the
Incas is not the same thing as the destruction of their
civilization. That empire was nothing but a "universal
state," that is, according to his own system, a late
incident in the disintegration of a civilization which
had already broken down. After that "Indian summer" winter had to come. With the additional help
of an interpretation of the oracle of archaeological
finds Professor Toynbee concludes that the civiliza-

tion of the Andes had received its self-inflicted death blow, before ever the Spaniards came.[9]

As far as the two Central American civilizations are concerned, these found themselves in an earlier stage of the fatal downward course; they were still in their Time of Troubles, the universal state was only just coming into sight; but here too the irresistible process of decay through internal shortcomings of the civilizations themselves had already started.

It will be observed that Professor Toynbee introduces into his argument his own theoretical construction as an established datum. This method is open to grave objection. It will not carry along the reader who has preserved his independence towards the system. But even greater are the liberties the author allows himself with respect to the arrested and the abortive civilizations. What does it matter, he says of the first, whether it was the thrust of an alien hand that caused their final collapse? Had they been left to themselves, their ruin simply as a result of exhaustion would have been merely a question of time. That is, if one assumes their arrested equilibrium to be in fact so fatally unshakable as Professor Toynbee has been trying to make out! As for the latter category: "It is true," he says, "that in each of the four cases the intractable challenge has been

[9] IV, 105.

delivered by some human neighbor or rival or adversary. Yet this does not entitle us to pronounce that the abortive civilizations have been deprived of their prospect of life by an external act of violence. The truth may be that these miscarriages have been due to some inherent weakness in the embryos, and that the pre-natal shocks by which the miscarriages have been precipitated have simply brought this inherent weakness out." [10] After such subtle and speculative reasoning the author thinks himself justified in leaving the cases of arrested and abortive civilizations aside and concludes (concerning the American three as well he now no longer admits any doubt) that of the ruined civilizations only the Hittite and the Arabic appear to have met their end as the result of alien interference; and even here in the end he expresses some doubt.

I have retraced this argument, not only because it is a daring piece of special pleading, well fitted to put us on our guard against the entire work, but also in order to introduce the question: why is Professor Toynbee so anxious that civilizations should come to an end not through external violence but as the result of their own shortcomings? Obviously because the whole of his outlook postulates this view. The idea that the spirit should succumb to violence is distaste-

[10] IV, 114.

ful, it is to him a lowering of the grandiose drama of history.

Of course the scene of history lies thickly sown with cases of brute force triumphing over right, over delicate humanity, over innocence. In Professor Toynbee's six tomes one can indeed find a good many such discussed, especially when in Volume III he wants to illustrate the possibility of a "challenge" being too strong. But these cases are only nations or states, subsections of the large units which in his view are really the exponents of civilization. Although detesting the militarist, the conqueror, whose activities he considers to be one of the factors helping to wreck a civilization (that is, the conqueror's own; a little chapter of Volume IV is entitled "The Suicidalness of Militarism"), and letting no opportunity pass to bring out the transitory nature of military success and the retribution by which it is closely followed—he sacrifices national communities with equanimity.[11]

After this the fourth volume, as might be expected, deals with the internal causes leading to the breakdown of civilizations. The subdivision of these is extremely ingenious. No doubt the results of the ingenuity at times seem farfetched, but here as

[11] How unmethodical is his treatment of national as distinct from "civilization" phenomena will be discussed later.

everywhere one comes across very striking ideas and extraordinarily fine pages. A most interesting view of the nineteenth century, for instance, is given in a discussion of the illusions and miscalculations of Cobden, who was firmly convinced that democracy and industrialism would secure peace.[12]

One of the weaknesses through which a civilization can go to its ruin is according to Toynbee "the nemesis of creativity," the loss of flexibility, the exhaustion, the self-conceit, frequently following upon a creative effort. No doubt this is a fruitful idea, yet again it cannot bear the far-stretched systematization to which the author subjects it. I could demonstrate this by a number of points. I confine myself to one.

In the same section where he deals with cases of extreme nationalism—that is, in his view, the allowing oneself to be hypnotized by the achievements of a previous generation—Toynbee devotes a lengthy argument to the history of the Italian *risorgimento* in order to bring out the fact that this resuscitation of a people which had in past centuries played so glorious a part was in reality confined to a region which had no share in that earlier achievement. Venice especially, he wants to show, was still too much under the spell of the memory of its glorious

[12] IV, 131 f.

past to co-operate effectively in the movement which was to make Italy free and one; but the same is true, according to him, of all the ancient city-states which had in the old days stood at the head of Western civilization, of Milan, Florence, Genoa. So it came about that a new country took the lead, Savoy-Piedmont, which had once as an old feudal territory let itself be passed by the astonishing social and cultural development of these now nerveless towns, but which for that very reason was at this juncture able to show such freshness and such energy.

This belongs to a class of explanations often loosely offered by historians: explanations which, when gone into a little more carefully, take so much for granted about the secret workings of the communal life of mankind as to stand in need themselves of elaborate elucidation. In the ordinary course, however, they are not gone into carefully, nor as a rule has the author himself so much as thought of the problems he fails to discuss. Of the same sort is the favorite remark, when an obscure phenomenon presents itself, that it springs from the *nature* of a particular people, this being itself an entity incapable of exact observation or definition. This kind of explanation merely begs the question. The interesting thing about Professor Toynbee is that not only has he carefully systematized a number of such theories, but has attempted with subtle historical arguments to demonstrate them. We have, however, already come across several instances of the attempt collapsing completely at the touch of independent criticism.

It makes admirable reading, this paragraph.[13] One follows the author with the excitement with which one watches an incredibly supple and audacious tightrope-walker. One feels inclined to exclaim: "C'est magnifique, mais ce n'est pas l'histoire." The grace, the daring with which the facts are handled are astonishing, the capacity of coining striking phrases uncommon. What a knowledge, what a wealth of general cultural backgrounds, how splendid the characterization of the new, non-Italian-Renaissance, feudal society of Savoy-Piedmont! But at the same time what the author leaves unsaid is at least as important and essential as what he mentions, and by its means one can reveal his thesis in its incompleteness, arbitrariness and untenability.

I cannot touch upon all the points I might query. There is a fascinating description of the deadness which had overtaken eighteenth-century Venice; but the explanation that all energy had been used up in the senseless attempt, inspired by faith in tradition, to keep alive a Mediterranean empire against the Turkish attacks, and that the lightheartedness and

[13] IV, 278–289.

frivolity of Venetian life were nothing but the psychological counterpart to that grim effort, seems to me one-sided. Was there really a large percentage of the Venetian aristocracy that bled in the Turkish wars? Should not the author have said at least a word about the concentration of all power in the hands of a tiny group from amongst that aristocracy? For it can hardly be doubted that this left a mark on the minds of the rest, just as the weaknesses of the eighteenth-century French nobility are in part to be explained by the setting up of an administrative apparatus in which they had no share. And when Professor Toynbee contrasts the bright colors of an English flag flying from a ship in a Canaletto painting with the muffled tones of the setting formed by the harbor of Venice, should he not have recalled the discovery of the sea route round the Cape of Good Hope and of America, and the displacement of trade from the Mediterranean to the Atlantic Ocean?

How is it—to confine myself to the chief point in Professor Toynbee's argument—that it was precisely Savoy-Piedmont which proved itself capable of that great political feat, the unification of Italy? He examines only the events of 1848–49. In that crisis Milan and Venice, both of which rose against Austrian rule, exhibited the greatest heroism, Savoy-Piedmont's military performance against Austria was on the contrary far from distinguished. "Yet this Piedmontese disgrace proved more fruitful for Italy than those Milanese and Venetian glories"; ten years and seventeen years later the work of liberation was performed (in conjunction with the French, it is true) by the Piedmontese army, while Milan and Venice remained passive. "The explanation is that the Venetian and Milanese exploits in 1848 were virtually foredoomed to failure, however magnificent they might be in their intrinsic worth, because the spiritual driving force behind them was still that idolization of their own dead selves, as historic mediaeval city-states, which had been defeating the finest efforts of Italian heroism and Italian statesmanship since the time of Machiavelli." [14]

"The explanation is. . . ." Apart from other considerations so simplistic a view rouses in the historian an instinctive distrust, which is not lessened by the apodictical delivery. "The nineteenth century Venetians," Professor Toynbee continues, "who responded to Manin's call in 1848 were fighting for Venice alone, and not for Piedmont or Milan or even for Padua; they were striving to restore an obsolete Venetian Republic and not to create a new Italian national state; and for this reason their enterprise was a forlorn hope, whereas Piedmont could survive a more shame-

[14] IV, 287.

ful disaster because the nineteenth-century Piedmontese were not fast bound in the misery and iron
of an unforgettable historic past." It should be
noticed that our author no longer makes any mention
of Milan. And indeed in Milan the rebels had formed
a "provisional government" which set itself no other
object but fusion with Piedmont on the one side and
with Venice on the other. In Milan at least it appears
to have been possible to get away from the fascination of the historic past, and the freedom of spiritual
movement which Professor Toynbee observes in the
new land of Piedmont was not so unique as he wants
to make us believe.

But when even the Venice revolt is examined more
closely, it will appear how lacking in the complexity
of life is his presentation of the facts. Manin had pro-
claimed the Republic at Venice; but he had done so
before the rising of Milan and the advance of Carlo
Alberto of Savoy-Piedmont were known there; the
Piedmontese consul himself had given his approval
to the decision.[15] Nor did Manin ever conceal his
opinion that the unity of Italy must be the final goal.
It is true that Manin resisted the pressure which was
soon put on him from Piedmont, and even from
Milan, to let Venice be merged into the Piedmontese

[15] G. M. Trevelyan, *Manin and the Venetian Republic of 1848*,
139.

kingdom without delay. It goes without saying that he was afterwards severely blamed for this by Italian historians who, after the bad habit of historians, used the event as the measure of all things; but if one looks at the circumstances of the moment, there is something to be said for his attitude. In any case it is incorrect to put forward a historically conditioned particularism as his only motive, or even to assert that he could not do otherwise because the Venetians would not have followed him. The Italian idea lived in Venice. But at the same time there were feelings of suspicion with respect to Carlo Alberto, feelings which were shared by Manin himself; his ability to live up to his promises was doubted. Especially that proud slogan *L'Italia farà da se,* behind which in reality there lurked the King's fear for the French revolution, was objected to in Venice. Manin and his friends realized that nothing could be achieved without France. And as a matter of fact in the end the great aim was only achieved with France. Could not the question why Italy's liberation failed to emerge from the heroic initiative of Milan and Venice in 1848, be answered thus: *The explanation is* that feudal Piedmont under a reactionary King was striving not so much after Italian unity as after the expansion of Piedmont, and in particular that this king rejected the help of revolutionary France? The state-

ment would surely be no more one-sided than the
solution presented to us by Professor Toynbee, his
imagination afire with that striking idea of "the nemesis of creativity." For although our author of course
imagines he is proceeding empirically here also, of
true empiricism, of an objective observation of the
facts, whatever the conclusions they may suggest,
this passage again is hardly an example.

There are still so many data which have been neglected! Savoy-Piedmont was able to play its great
part, even after the failure of 1848–49, because it
was independent and moreover was by its situation
in a better position than any other Italian region to
co-operate with France. These simple facts might at
least have been mentioned before the Middle Ages
were called in to explain the failures or the passivity
of Milan and Venice. Piedmont was certainly not the
strongest spiritual radiating center of the new Italian
sentiment. Alfieri, who dreamt of Italy in an earlier
generation, was a Piedmontese, but "dépiémontisé"; [16]
Massimo d'Azeglio, one of the great intellectual as
well as political leaders of the *risorgimento*, also
came from Piedmont, but he was married in Milan,
where he lived for many years; without the Milanese
atmosphere he would not have been the man he became. Silvio Pellico and Leopardi were Milanese.

[16] Henri Hauvette, *Littérature Italienne* (1914), 383.

Garibaldi was a native of Nice, which belonged to Piedmont, but it was as a sailor and outside Piedmont that he became acquainted with the Italian idea. Mazzini came from Genoa, and Genoa was one of those towns with a great past, which had in fact offered embittered opposition to annexation to Piedmont in 1815. Mazzini, the prophet of the unitary Italian Republic, had his following scattered over the whole central and northern portions of the peninsula, but in monarchical Piedmont it was perhaps weakest. The older *Carbonari* were merged with his new organization *La giovine Italia:* those pioneers of Italian unity again had certainly not been most numerous in Piedmont. But all this is passed by in silence by Professor Toynbee, which is, it must be admitted, the most convenient method when one wants to subject history to a system.

I shall make one more remark—out of many which present themselves—and this because I can here invoke Professor Toynbee himself. In those years 1848–49 there happened another sensational event, the rising in Rome, the proclamation of the Republic there, and the resistance led by Mazzini and Garibaldi against the French army besieging the town. In Volume II Professor Toynbee assures us that Rome's heroic perseverance, even though it ended in defeat, made the profoundest impression on the national imagination.[17] He there mentions the incident merely to argue that it supplied the decisive consideration for the choice, later on, of Rome as capital of the new Italy—in itself a disputable view: was it not the fact of Rome appearing on the strength of her ancient glory predestined for that position which had inspired Mazzini and Garibaldi to plant their banner there? But however that may be, in his second volume Professor Toynbee gives to Rome's behavior in the crisis of 1848–49 an emphasis which makes it all the more remarkable that, two volumes later, intent only on bringing out the providential part played by the new land of Piedmont, he has not a word to say about it.

6

Volumes V and VI are concerned with the process of disintegration, that fatal downgrade course to which a broken-down civilization is irretrievably committed. I shall not continue subjecting passages to detailed criticism: the examples already tested will have to suffice. I shall rather try to survey the system itself and discuss one or two chief points.

Professor Toynbee himself furnishes his readers with announcements and repetitions or summaries, and it is thus easy to survey the system. It all appears

[17] II, 400–1.

to fit together closely and precisely. But when we try to apply it to the multiform world of reality we fare like little Alice at the croquet game in Wonderland. The mallet turns out to be a flamingo, which twists its long neck the moment we want to strike; the ball is a hedgehog, which unrolls itself and runs off; while for hoops there are doubled-up soldiers, who rise to their full height and get together for a chat just when you are aiming in their direction.

"In a growing civilization, as we have seen," Professor Toynbee writes in his sixth volume,[18] "a creative personality comes into action by taking the lead in making a successful response to some challenge. . . . In a disintegrating civilization Challenge and Response is still the mould of action in which the mystery of creation takes place, but . . . [while] in a growing civilization the creator is called upon to play the part of a conqueror who replies to a challenge with a victorious response, in a disintegrating society the same creator is called upon to play the part of a savior who comes to the rescue of a society that has failed to respond because the challenge has worsted a minority that has ceased to be creative and has sunk to be merely dominant. . . . A growing society is taking the offensive . . . [and wants its leader] to capture fresh ground for its advance, whereas a dis-

[18] VI, 177.

integrating society is trying to stand on the defensive and therefore requires its leader to play the more thankless . . . part of a savior who will show it how to hold its ground in a rearguard action."

"As we have seen." Is that indeed what we have seen, and are we in the two latest volumes seeing the rest? As for me, no! Undoubtedly, I have been shown leading or creative personalities in one and the other function; I had indeed seen the like before. But how do I know that the difference is caused by the triumphant creator acting in a growing society and the hopelessly struggling one in a society in disintegration? I have not been convinced of the essential difference between the phases of civilization, and still less have I been convinced that a period of growth is by a breakdown irretrievably cut off, so that the stricken civilization, with its "members," the creative minds included, must from then on have got on to the fatal slope which will carry it to its ruin in three beats and a half and in an unknown number of centuries—irretrievably, with this qualification however, which can hardly be considered a mercy, that it may stay somewhere suspended between life and death in a state of petrifaction.[19] To me, even after the fourth volume of Professor Toynbee, this great event of the breakdown, which is supposed to lead

[19] V, 2; 22.

to the fatal process, remains a mystery; and after his third and fifth and sixth volumes the conceptions of growth and of disintegration retain so much that is fluid, vague and uncertain that I find it difficult to use them for the subdivision of history, especially in conformity with his rigid system. I can sympathize more with the modesty of Huizinga, who, in comparing successive centuries of civilization, came to the conclusion that the conception of "a rising civilization" will escape us as soon as we attempt to apply it: "the height of a civilization cannot be measured." I know very well that these are no more than very simple remarks occurring in an unpretentious essay [20] and that they are very far from exhausting the subject. But when placed beside Professor Toynbee's omniscient positiveness, they seem to me instinct with profound wisdom.

It is noteworthy that our author himself, after having written two heavy volumes about disintegration, and after having in every imaginable way subdivided and analyzed and even tabulated [21] the phe-

[20] *"Geschonden Wereld,"* published posthumously in 1945. Huizinga is here arguing against the believers in a continuous progress of our own civilization, a group to which Professor Toynbee does not of course belong. But his remarks are relevant also against Toynbee's pretention to indicate (as he attempts to do in Volume VI) the exact *rhythm* of all civilizations.

[21] These tables—four in all—are to be found among the appendices to Volume VI, p. 327 ff. The way in which Western civilization is there dealt with might give rise to an extensive critical

nomenon, cannot tell us whether we are experiencing it at this moment. In order to explain that uncertainty he regales us with a wealth of metaphor, yet it remains curious. At first glance one should think that the two phases of growth and of disintegration, as sketched by the author himself, present a contrast like that between day and night, which cannot remain hidden from the observation of contemporaries. The creative personalities in a growing society triumphantly find the right answer, and the new challenge to which this gives rise with its once more triumphant response can be compared to the taking possession of fresh territory. There you have growth; while on the other hand in a disintegrating society the leaders are doomed to a veritable sisyphean labor. At best a respite can be gained, but after every apparent victory there follows a worse setback. And

discussion. I shall do no more than make a few remarks on the first table. The first thing that strikes one is that Western civilization is there unquestioningly drafted into a table particularizing the disintegration process. It is surprising, and not in agreement with remarks made elsewhere in the book, to see the Time of Troubles fixed for the Western half between 1378 and 1797 and for the Eastern half between 1128 and 1528. Two universal states are indicated, the Napoleonic empire and the Danubian monarchy. When in connection therewith one sees a *pax oecumenica* assigned to the years 1797–1814 and 1528–1918 respectively, one is inclined to ask if words have the same meaning for Professor Toynbee as they have for the rest of us.—Of the other tables I shall only say that they too seem to show to excess the author's gift of observing parallels and of building constructions on them.

we, who may have been living in that wretched condition for the last four centuries (for that is the possibility suggested by Professor Toynbee)—should we
not know it?

There is an indication here that the author is less
rigid and doctrinaire in the application than in the
exposition of his system. The instances in which this
appears can be brought up against him to show him
in contradiction with himself. They can also be
placed to his credit. In any case the fact remains that
innumerable remarks and illustrations scattered over
the six volumes do not agree too well with the strict
lines of the system, but at the same time contribute
not a little to the color and the fascination of the
work. Especially when our Western civilization is
under discussion can this be observed.

He seeks, for instance, to establish the existence in
our Western society of a proletariat (in his sense of
the word) and of a dominating minority, and of other
equivalents of phenomena belonging typically to the
disintegration process in civilizations which he indicates have run their course to final dissolution. There
are, to mention only a few points, the loss of style, the
aping of alien and barbaric forms of art, the tendencies to archaism and futurism. I have no room to
follow his disquisitions on all these points. I will
only say that they are frequently stimulating to the

highest degree, but that as frequently they leave one
completely unsatisfied. Wide prospects seem to be
opened by his discussion of the danger threatening
our civilization from the sudden assimilation of large
areas with other cultural traditions, with all the consequences of "standardization" and leveling.[22] On
the other hand the discussion of the twin tendencies
of archaism and futurism strikes me as disappointing,
meagre, and so incomplete as to become lopsided. To
bring National Socialism and Fascism under the
heading "archaism" is to belittle the historical significance of these evil doctrines overmuch. And is it
possible to overlook the fact that both archaism and
futurism can be considered disintegration phenomena
only in excess, that both are among the indispensable
forms of life of any civilization, of a growing civilization as well, that they need each other and are often
found together?

But there is one point to which I want especially to
draw attention. In the theoretical development of his
system Professor Toynbee poses a dilemma: a civilization is either in growth or it is in disintegration.
When, therefore, one sees him noting so many grave
symptoms in our Western history, one is surprised at
his leaving open the question as to the stage in which
we find ourselves. But he also mentions phenomena

[22] V, 89; 153.

as occurring in our modern history which *per definitionem* belong to the period of growth. It is sufficient to recall the (in certain respects somewhat fantastic) description of England as a creative minority living in retirement and of the great achievements resulting therefrom. I do not see how to solve these contradictions. But I am quite willing to rejoice that Professor Toynbee does not in practice keep growth and disintegration so strictly separate as might be expected from his program. Could we but lay aside his system, with its precise subdivisions and sequences, we could find in his analyses and parallels, in his interpretations and even in his terminology, so much to stimulate thought and to activate the imagination!

But of course the system, the doctrine, belongs to the essence of the work, and we cannot after all do without it if we want to follow Toynbee in his reflections upon our own civilization. We shall have to wait for the twelfth part before we see his diagnosis and his prognosis concerning it fully expounded, but in the meantime he has repeatedly touched upon the subject. The element of uniformity in the rhythm of the disintegration process, he says,[23] looking back on his own examination of the histories of the most widely varied civilizations, "is apparently so definite and so constant that, on the strength of its regularity,

[23] VI, 321.

we have almost ventured to cast the horoscope of one civilization that is still alive and on the move." Even more suggestive is the passage in which he toys with the possibility—for here again he refrains from speaking positively—of Western civilization having broken down as long ago as the wars of religion of the sixteenth century. The minds of some readers instinctively revolt against the idea of our possibly being caught up in a disintegration fatally proceeding to ruin or petrifaction. So Toynbee's disintegration theory has been misread, and by some of his most fervent admirers who were fain to think that even in case we are already broken-down he still leaves us the hope of finding "the right answer." [24] But this is not so. For Professor Toynbee everything turns upon the question: has the breakdown actually taken place, or not?

At first glance one is inclined to say: how is it possible to single out the sixteenth-century wars of religion as having such fatal significance? Indeed to me the suggestion that our Time of Troubles began with them seems unacceptable. There really had been no lack of wars in the preceding centuries, not even of socially destructive wars: the crusade against the Albigensians, the Hundred Years' War, to mention only these.

[24] Professor Romein in *De Nieuwe Stem* (1946), 44.

But for Professor Toynbee the evil thing about the wars of religion is their being wars of *religion*. He is struck not only by the rending asunder of Christendom, but by the atrocious paradox that from the highest good, from the belief in the one God, there was distilled that suicidal poison of intolerance. (Of course, without leaving the plane of his argument, one might remind him of the fact, with which he is certainly familiar, that even this was far from being a new development, although undoubtedly so violent an explosion of religious hatred had never before ranged the Christian nations in opposing camps.) Suspecting that it was these events that marked the beginning of our Time of Troubles, our Christian philosopher finds confirmation in the fact that the appeasement he observes in the third quarter of the seventeenth century proceeded, not from the only true motive, the religious—not from the recognition of all religions as a search for the one spiritual aim— but from an even more cynical temper than that which in the fourth century had underlain the religious toleration policy of the Roman Empire, from weariness and indifference, from *raison d'état*. When Professor Toynbee describes the principle of *cuius regio eius religio* as "a monstrously cynical principle," [25] he knows exactly what he means—even though

[25] For this and preceding utterances cf. IV, 221, 225, 228.

the question may well be asked whether justice is done to that age by a judgment based so wholly on later considerations. The expulsion of the Huguenots from France long after the termination of the Wars of Religion was a particularly barbaric application of this same principle; but even the milder forms of the Caesaropapism which was now in the ascendant, of that domination of the lower over the higher, have, so the argument continues, weakened the foundations of our civilization. The barbaric, the despotic aspects were not the worst, or rather from them sprang, as a fatal consequence, a new factor leading straight to the abyss, namely, scepticism, contempt for religion.

"In our time," he writes in an Annex to Volume V, "this repudiation of a spiritual principle which is no doubt exposed, in human hearts, to the danger of being poisoned or perverted, but which is none the less the breath of human life, has been carried to such lengths in all parts of a Westernized 'Great Society' that it is beginning at last to be recognized for what it is. It is being recognized, that is to say, as the supreme danger to the spiritual health and even to the material existence of the Western body social—a deadlier danger, by far, than any of our hotly canvassed and loudly advertised political and economic maladies."

Here we have, I think, the hard core of Professor Toynbee's view of history. In this spirit it is no doubt possible—although really I am now anticipating that twelfth part which we may not receive from his hands for a number of years—to construct a downward line with the sixteenth-century religious wars as a point of departure.

Must that line infallibly lead to the final catastrophe? According to the system, undoubtedly. I merely remind you of the cases of the three ancient American civilizations which were apparently in disintegration and whose ruin was therefore, according to Professor Toynbee, so wholly a question of time that he will not admit the forcible interference of the Spaniards as proof that a civilization can be destroyed by an external power. And yet . . . now that our own civilization is involved, he too seems to shrink back from the iron consistency of his fatalistic construction. On this point as well the published volumes contain several indications as to what he is likely to say about the problem in his promised fuller treatment. There is in particular a passage in Volume V, whose splendid eloquence comes straight from the heart.[26]

His starting-point is "the miracle" of the conversion of the Negro slaves in America to their masters'

[26] V, 193–4.

ancestral religion. Here, he says, "we can see the familiar schism between the Proletariat and the Dominant Minority being healed in our Western body social by a Christianity which our dominant minority has been trying to repudiate." "The eighteenth century Methodist preachers who sowed that seed . . . were at the same time converting . . . the neglected slum-dwellers in . . . Wales and Northern England. . . . In our post-war generation [the writer is of course referring to the generation after the *First* World War], in which the lately brilliant prospects of a neo-pagan dominant minority have been rapidly growing dim, the sap of life is visibly flowing once again through all the branches of our Western Christendom; and this spectacle suggests that perhaps, after all, the next chapter in our Western history may not follow the lines of the final chapter in the history of Hellenism. Instead of seeing some new church spring from the ploughed-up soil of an internal proletariat in order to serve as the executor and residuary legatee of a civilization that has broken down and gone into disintegration, we may yet live to see a civilization which has tried and failed to stand alone, being saved, in spite of itself, from a fatal fall by being caught in the arms of an ancestral church which it has vainly striven to push away and keep at arm's length. . . . Is such a spiritual re-birth possible?

If we put Nicodemus' question, we may take his instructor's answer." The reference is to John, III: "Marvel not that I have said unto thee, ye must be born again.—The wind bloweth where it listeth, and thou hearest the sound thereof, but canst not tell whence it cometh and whither it goeth: so is every one that is born of the Spirit."

What is the meaning of this? It means that Professor Toynbee in his heart believes that our civilization has fallen a prey to the disintegration process; but in spite of the inexorable sentence which therefore according to his system holds sway over us, he leaves us one possibility yet: the grace of a conversion, or of a return, to faith.

7

Professor Toynbee does not address himself to fellow-believers only. Occasionally he alludes to the "neo-pagan" intellectuals of the modern world in a tone of mild sarcasm, at times a little less mild, although not unmixed with pity. But in at least one passage he invites them into the circle of men of good will as rightful claimants to a share in the Western cultural inheritance. His *method* at any rate is not intended to be that of the religious prophet. Utterances from which it appears that he expects salvation from faith only, drop from him out of the fullness of his heart, but as it were in passing. His method he presents as empirical.

Now the last question I want to examine is—what has this method to give us for the better understanding of the history and the inextricably related present-day problem of our own Western civilization? That Toynbee's system is to me unacceptable I have already stated clearly enough. But his work contains more than the system. Does his method, which undeniably yields striking results every now and again, promise an important contribution to that subject which concerns us all so closely?

It is perhaps unfair to the author if, in conclusion, and after so much criticism, I confine myself to expounding two objections to his method in this particular connection. Let me at least remark with some emphasis that, in spite of all that may be urged against it, the work here too is immensely stimulating, and that the volume in which his views on our own troubles and prospects will at last be systematically set forth promises to be profoundly interesting. But on two points I shall advance a formulation of my doubts.

If Professor Toynbee has not so far given a set analysis of this particular subject, in his own opinion the comparison with the other civilizations whose course he *has* investigated is already of the greatest importance for the right understanding of what we are living through ourselves. In a certain sense this is a thesis no one will contest. An insight into any historical process trains the mind for the grasping of other processes. But Professor Toynbee's idea is that it is permissible to conclude from analogies, and to this view, which underlies the whole of his work, I shall now, at this late stage, without absolutely rejecting it, attach a label, "Handle with caution."

I am not going to attempt an examination of the problem in its full extent and its first principles. I shall only point out that, generally speaking, parallels in history, however indispensable and frequently instructive, are never wholly satisfactory, because each phenomenon is embedded in its own circumstances, never to be repeated, from which it cannot be completely detached. This warning must be especially taken to heart by anyone setting out to compare this civilization of ours with other and older civilizations. The circumstances have in many ways undergone so profound a change that we seem to be living in another world from the ancient Egyptians, or the ancient Chinese, or Iranians, or whatever peoples provide Professor Toynbee with his rules and laws, in another world also from that of the Hellenized Romans, whose decline and fall have obviously strongly influenced his mind in the construction of his system.

I realize perfectly that *he* will be little accessible to this consideration. His view of history is pre-eminently a spiritual one. I am far from being a believer in historical materialism, but for all that I do not think that material changes can, in this argument, be simply ignored. Book-printing; telegraph, telephone, radio; incredibly increased speed of transport; productive capacity immensely heightened; unfortunately also powers of destruction raised to an unheard-of degree—all this has created conditions which have not left the processes of spiritual life uninfluenced and on which the possibilities of development and degeneration, the tendencies and powers of resistance of our present-day society are to such an extent dependent that it must be a particularly ticklish undertaking to draw its horoscope, as Professor Toynbee puts it, from the experiences of earlier ages.

The other point is concerned with one particular shortcoming which I seem to discern in Professor Toynbee's disquisitions on our civilization, his attitude towards the national varieties within the wider unit of Western civilization. I have already remarked upon the unruffled serenity with which, while insisting so strongly on the impotence of external violence with respect to his "civilizations," he accepts the cases without number in which violence has triumphed over national communities. National independence inspires him with distrust, national ambitions he rejects. He does not really do justice to the historical reality of national life, of national desire for self-preservation or even for expansion.

A striking instance is to be found in his treatment of the downfall of the Boer Republics in 1902. In his view the statesmen of the British Empire were driven to make use of their overwhelming military superiority because the national ambitions of the two backward independent miniature states made their preservation inconsistent with any other solution; and indeed, at the cost of a small local war, it proved possible subsequently to pursue a constructive policy within the Empire, which gave satisfaction to Dutch nationalism. A surprisingly idyllic presentation of the episode! Surprising especially as coming from this same Professor Toynbee who is so much governed by the idiosyncrasy of the apostle of gentleness that he attaches the name of "hangman" to the conqueror as representative of a dominant minority—and this with Caesar for an example! [27]

The fact is that this particular idiosyncrasy of his is here overruled by that of the hater of nationalism. It is under that heading, or in his terminology under the heading of "the idolization of an ephemeral self,"

[27] V, 138.

one of the mental attitudes leading to the breakdown of civilizations, that the South African case is
cited.[28] The writer's opinion, by the way, that it
presents a contrast with that of Ireland, where the
nationalists go on fostering their hatred of England,
and with that of Servia, which caused the dissolution
of the Austro-Hungarian monarchy, is an error. The
cult of superannuated grievances and the raising of
particular rights to the level of the absolute, which
are characteristic of a wronged nationalism, certainly
belong to the dreariest and most dangerous phenomena of the modern age; Professor Toynbee
sketches them in the cases with which he is acquainted with the insight born of loathing. But when
he asserts that South Africa has now become a peace-
able multi-national state, after the pattern of Switzerland, and that this proves a new country to possess
a greater psychological plasticity as compared with
the petrifaction in its obsessions characteristic of
old Europe, this only shows, as do other passages
also,[29] that he is not well informed about the Afrik-

[28] IV, 295.
[29] There is in particular a passage in which Afrikaans as a
cultural language is belittled in comparison with Dutch: V, 493–4.
It is amusing to see so completely misinformed a statement delivered so positively. Of course not even Professor Toynbee can
know everything. It is useful, nevertheless, quite apart from the
considerations built upon it in the text, to note such mistakes. The
conclusion may be drawn that it is not imperative to believe

ander national movement. These mistakes spring from, or at least are not unconnected with, this same inability to appreciate nationalism; perhaps it is wiser to avoid that ambiguous word in -ism and to say that Professor Toynbee here shows in small things the same lack of understanding for the reality of the national factor in history.

This constitutes one of the serious shortcomings of the entire work. If the destructiveness of nationalism when driven to extremes by oppression or even by fancied wrongs is an undeniable fact, it still cannot be overlooked—although Professor Toynbee does overlook it—that in the cultural construction of our Western world national foundations are of essential importance. This does not in the least amount to throwing doubts on the reality of the greater civilization of which the European nations, to use Professor Toynbee's word, are "members." But we are faced by a problem here which is not to be solved by a one-sided negation. In the very first of Professor Toynbee's volumes he placed himself in an untenable position. It is all to the good that the writers of national histories should be reminded that their subject does not form a self-contained whole, that it has to take

---

him unreservedly when he speaks with the same assurance about peoples or ages unfamiliar to us and constructs his towering conclusions on facts which we cannot so easily check.

its place, and this without any well-marked delimita-
tion, in a greater whole. It is all to the good to make
an attempt to survey the greatest whole of all, so that
the sense of the dependence of the parts may not
only be strengthened but may take shape. When,
however, Professor Toynbee considers himself so
far superior to the distinction between "parochial
states" as to ridicule professorial colleagues who set
the diplomatic relations between two of these
ephemeral units as thesis subjects, he exaggerates not
a little. And when he poses the civilization, in the
sense of one of the twenty-one, as the smallest "intelligible field of historical study," he is putting forward an impossible, an impracticable demand.

I have pointed out that he himself every now and
again, when speaking not only of our own Western
Civilization but also for instance of the Hellenic,
cites phenomena which are particularist or national.
This is of course quite inevitable. But since he has
done nothing but belittle the national factor instead
of accurately defining its relationship to the larger
whole, he is all the time coming into conflict with his
own impossibly universalist system. Wherever possible he adduces examples of "parochial" phenomena
as illustrations of the tendencies of a civilization in
its entirety. This is certainly a great convenience to
him in his arguments: it becomes easy in this way

to prove anything. Our Western Civilization in particular offers a rich variety of choice. It is only once or twice that he so much as mentions the problem, and not many of his readers will go along with him when he extends an observation made in the case of one people without further ado to cover all.

The case in question is that of National Socialism in Germany.[30] "Germany's troubles in the present generation can be ascribed, without dispute, to the contemporary Zeitgeist of the Western Society of which Germany herself is a fraction." The "without dispute" does not make the statement any more convincing. In another passage he even writes: "Italy and Germany are no alien appendages to the Western body social; they are bone of its bone and flesh of its flesh; and it follows that the social revolution which has taken place yesterday in Italy and Germany under our eyes may overtake us in France or England or the Netherlands or Scandinavia tomorrow." The thesis I accept unhesitatingly; but the conclusion seems to me unjustified. Why? Because, apart from the cohesion of the large civilization area, there is the variety of national traditions, of national history. These it is that settle the question whether tendencies which will no doubt be present in several countries, without however constituting

[30] VI, 57, footnote.

the whole of the *Zeitgeist,* will in one particular country gain the ascendancy or not. His unwillingness to recognize this fact, by which nevertheless in practice his argument is repeatedly ruled, his failure to make up his mind about this, one of the chief problems of the Western civilization area, strikes me as a serious weakness.

Considering this, taking it together with the doubtful applicability of his comparisons—doubtful especially in this particular case—I can, after all the other indications as to the necessity of caution, have little confidence any longer that Professor Toynbee, when later on he undertakes a set examination of our civilization and its prospects, will prove able to enlighten our perplexities; or should I not rather say that we need not let ourselves be frightened by his darkness? We need not accept his view that the whole of modern history from the sixteenth century on has been nothing but a downward course, following the path of rout and rally. We need not let ourselves be shaken in our confidence that the future lies open before us, that in the midst of misery and confusion such as have so frequently occurred in history, we still dispose of forces no less valuable than those by which earlier generations have managed to struggle through their troubles.

Can We Know the Pattern of the Past?

Discussion between

PIETER GEYL *and* ARNOLD J. TOYNBEE

PROFESSOR GEYL

THE SIX VOLUMES of Toynbee's *Study of History* appeared before the war, but it is since the war that the book and the author have become famous. A generation only just recovering from the terrible experiences of the war and already anxious about the future, is reading the work in the hope of finding in its pages the answer to its perplexities. It is indeed the author's claim to discover for us, in the at first sight chaotic and confusing spectacle of human history, a pattern, a rhythm. . . .

I must come straight to the main features of the system. Has Toynbee proved that the histories of civilizations fall into these sharply marked stages of growth and disintegration, separated by breakdown? Has he proved that the work of the creative minds, or of the creative minorities, can be successful only in the first stage and that in the second it is doomed to remain so much fruitless effort?

In my opinion he has not. How do I know that the difference is caused by the triumphant creator acting in a growing society, and the hopelessly struggling one in a society in disintegration? I have not been convinced of the essential difference between the phases of civilization. There are evil tendencies and there are good tendencies simultaneously present at every stage of human history, and the human intellect is not sufficiently comprehensive to weigh them off against each other and to tell, before the event, which is to have the upper hand. As for the theory that the individual leader, or the leading minority, is capable of creative achievement in a growing society only and doomed to disappointment in one that is in disintegration—that theory lapses automatically when the distinction is not admitted in the absolute form in which our author propounds it.

I am glad that you are present here, Toynbee, and going to reply. For this is surely a point of great practical importance. *A Study of History* does not definitely announce ruin as did Spengler's book by its very title. But in more than one passage you give us to understand that Western civilization broke down as long ago as the sixteenth century, as a result of the wars of religion. The last four centuries of our history would thus, according to your system, be one long process of disintegration, with collapse as the inevitable end—except for the miracle of a reconversion to the faith of our fathers.

There is no doubt, when we look around us, a great deal to induce gloom. But I do not see any reason why history should be read so as to deepen our sense of uneasiness into a mood of hopelessness. Earlier generations have also had their troubles and have managed to struggle through. There is nothing in history to shake our confidence that the future lies open before us.

PROFESSOR TOYNBEE

The fate of the world—the destiny of mankind— *is* involved in the issue between us about the nature of history.

In replying to Professor Geyl now, I am going to concentrate on what, to my mind, are his two main lines of attack. One of his general criticisms is: "Toynbee's view of history induces gloom." The other is: "Toynbee has set himself to do something impossible. He is trying to make sense of human history, and that is beyond the capacity of the human mind." I will pay most attention to this second point, because it is, I am sure, by far the more important of the two.

Let me try to dispose of the "gloom" point first. Suppose my view of history did point to a gloomy conclusion, what of it? "Gloomy" and "cheerful" are one thing, "true" and "false" quite another.

Professor Geyl has interpreted me rightly in telling you that I have pretty serious misgivings about the state of the world today. Don't you feel the same misgivings? Doesn't Professor Geyl feel them? That surely goes without saying. But what doesn't go without saying is what we are going to do about it; and here Professor Geyl has been handsome to me in telling you where I stand. He has told you that I disbelieve in predestination and am at the opposite pole, on that supremely important question, from the famous German philosopher Spengler. He has told you that my outlook is the reverse of historical materialism; that, in my view, the process of civilization is one of vanquishing the material problems to grapple with the spiritual ones; that I am a believer in free will; in man's freedom to respond with all his heart and soul and mind when life presents him with a challenge. Well, that is what I do believe. But how, I ask you, can one lift up one's heart and apply one's mind unless one does one's best to find out the relevant facts and to look them in the face?—the formidable facts as well as the encouraging ones.

In the state of the world today, the two really formidable facts, as I see them, are that the other civilizations that we know of have all broken down, and that in our recent history one sees some of those tendencies which, in the histories of the broken-down civilizations, have been the obvious symptoms of breakdown. But what's the moral? Surely not to shy at the facts. Professor Geyl himself admits them. And also, surely, not to be daunted by the "sense of uneasiness" which these formidable facts are bound to give us. "I don't see any reason," said Professor Geyl just now, "why history should be read so as to deepen our sense of uneasiness into a mood of hopelessness." That is a telling criticism of Spengler, who does diagnose that our civilization is doomed, and who has nothing better to suggest than that we should fold our hands and await the inevitable blow of the axe. But that ball doesn't take my wicket, for in my view, as Geyl has told you, uneasiness is a challenging call to action, and not a death sentence to paralyze our wills. Thank goodness we do know the fates of the other civilizations; such knowledge is a chart that warns us of the reefs ahead. Knowledge can be power and salvation if we have the spirit to use it. There is a famous Greek epigram which runs: "I am the tomb of a shipwrecked sailor, but don't let that frighten off you, brother mariner, from setting sail; because, when we went down, the other ships kept afloat."

"There is nothing in history," said Professor Geyl in his closing sentence, "to shake our confidence that the future lies open before us." Those might have been my own words, but I don't quite see what warrant Professor Geyl has for using them. The best comfort Professor Geyl can give us is: "If we take care not to unnerve ourselves by trying to chart the seas, we may be lucky enough to get by without hitting the rocks." No, I haven't painted him quite black enough, for his view is still gloomier than that. "To make a chart of history," he says, "is a sheer impossibility." Professor Geyl's own chart, you see, is the "perfect and absolute blank" of Lewis Carroll's bellman who hunted the snark. Geyl, too, has a chart, like Spengler and me. We all of us have one, whether we own up to it or not, and no chart is more than one man's shot at the truth. But surely, of those three, the blank is the most useless and the most dangerous.

Professor Geyl thinks I am a pessimist because I see a way of escape in a reconversion to the faith of our fathers. "This," says Professor Geyl, "is an unnecessarily gloomy view of our situation"—like the old lady who was advised to leave it to Providence and exclaimed: "Oh dear, has it come to that?"

What was our fathers' chart of history? As they saw it, it was a tale told by God, unfolding itself from the Creation through the Fall and the Redemption to the Last Judgment. As Professor Geyl says he sees it, it seems like a tale told by an idiot, signifying nothing. You may not agree with our fathers' view that history is a revelation of God's providence; but it is a poor exchange, isn't it, to swap their faith for the view that history makes no sense.

Of course, Professor Geyl is no more singular in his view than I am in mine. What one may call the nonsense view of history has been fashionable among Western historians for the last few generations. The odd thing is that some of the holders of this view—I don't know whether I could count Professor Geyl among the number—defend it principally on the ground that it is scientific. Of course, it is only human that historians should have wanted to be scientific in an age when science has been enjoying such prestige. I am, myself, a historian who believes that science has an awful lot to teach us. But how strange to suppose that one is being scientific by despairing of making sense! For what is science? It is only another name for the careful and scrupulous use of the human mind. And, if men despair of reason, they are lost. Nature hasn't given us wings, fur, claws, antennae or elephant's trunks; but she has given us the human intellect—the most effective of all implements, if we are not too timid to use it. And what does this scientific intellect do? It looks at the facts, but it doesn't stop there. It looks at the facts and it tries to make sense of them. It does, you see, the very thing that Professor Geyl takes me to task for trying to do with the facts of history.

Is history really too hard a nut for science to crack? When the human intellect has wrested her secret from physical nature, are we going to sit down under an *ex cathedra* dictum that the ambition to discover the secret of human history will always be bound to end in disappointment? We don't need to be told that Man is a harder—a very much harder—nut than the atom. We have discovered how to split the atom and are in danger of splitting it to our own destruction. By comparison with the science of physics, the science of man is so difficult that our discoveries in the two fields have gone forward at an uneven pace till they have got quite out of step with each other. It is partly this that has got us into our present fix. Is science to shirk trying to do anything about it? "The proper study of mankind is man," says Pope. "The human intellect," sighs Geyl, "is not sufficiently comprehensive."

I say: We can't afford such defeatism; it is unworthy of the greatness of man's mind; and it is refuted by the human mind's past achievements. The mind has won all its great victories by well-judged boldness. And today, before our eyes, science is launching a characteristically bold offensive in what is now the key area of the mental battlefield. Why, she has got her nutcrackers round this nut, this human nut, already. One arm of the pincers is the exciting young science of psychology, which is opening out entirely new mental horizons for us, in the very direction in which we are most in need of longer vistas. The other is the forbidding yet reward-ing discipline of statistics. Science has set herself now in good earnest to comprehend human nature, and, through understanding, to show it how to mas-ter itself and thereby to set itself free. Science, so long preoccupied with the riddles of non-human nature, has now joined in the quests of philosophy and reli-gion, and this diversion of her energies has been timely. There is, indeed, no time to be lost. We are in for a life-and-death struggle. And, at this critical hour, is science to get no support from our professedly scientific historians?

Well, in this "mental fight," I have deliberately risked my neck by putting my own reading of the facts of history on the table. I should never dream of claiming that my particular interpretation is the only one possible. There are, I am sure, many different alternative ways of analyzing history, each of which is true in itself and illuminating as far as it goes, just as, in dissecting an organism, you can throw light on its nature by laying bare either the skeleton or the muscles or the nerves or the circulation of the blood. No single one of these dissections tells the whole truth, but each of them reveals a genuine facet of it. I should be well content if it turned out that I had laid bare one genuine facet of history, and even then, I should measure my success by the speed with which my own work in my own line was put out of date by further work by other people in the same field. In the short span of one lifetime, the personal contribution of the individual scholar to the great and growing stream of knowledge can't be more than a tiny pailful. But if he could inspire—or provoke—other scholars to pour in their pailfuls too, well, then he could feel that he had really done his job. And this job of making sense of history is one of the crying needs of our day—I beg of you, believe me.

PROFESSOR GEYL

Well I must say, Toynbee, that I felt some anxiety while you were pouring out over me this torrent of eloquence, wit and burning conviction, but that was of course what I had to expect from you. And now that is over I'm relieved to feel that I'm still there, and my position untouched.

Professor Toynbee pictures me as one of those men who mistake the courage to see evils for gloom, and who when others sound the call for action take refuge from the dangers of our time in an illusionist optimism. But have I been saying that we are not in danger? And that no action is required? What I have said is that Toynbee's system induces the wrong kind of gloom because it tends to make action seem useless. "But I am a believer in man's free will," Toynbee replies. I know. But nevertheless, his system lays it down that the civilization which has been overtaken by a breakdown is doomed. Now Toynbee has repeatedly suggested that our Western civilization did suffer a breakdown as long ago as the sixteenth century, and that consequently, try as we may, we cannot avoid disaster. Except in one way, except in case we allow ourselves to be reconverted to the faith of our fathers. And here Toynbee exclaims: "You see, I'm not so gloomy after all." Perhaps not. But if one happens to hold a different opinion both of the efficacy and of the likelihood of application of his particular remedy, one cannot help thinking that Toynbee is but offering us cold comfort. He talks as if we cannot advance matters by "so hotly

canvassing and loudly advertising," as he contemptu-
ously puts it, "our political and economic maladies."
It is the loss of religious faith that is the deadly danger. To most of us this is indeed condemning all our
efforts to futility.

Of course, Toynbee, it is only your picturesque
way of putting things when you describe me as one
of those historians who cling to the nonsense view of
history. Because I cannot accept either your methods or your system it does not follow that to my
mind history has no meaning. I do not believe that
at any time it will be possible to reduce the past to
so rigid a pattern as to enable us to forecast the future—granted. Yet to me, as to you, the greatest
function of the historian is to interpret the past—to
find sense in it, although at the same time it is the
least scientific, the most inevitably subjective of his
functions.

I am surprised that you class me with those historians who believe that their view of history rests
securely on scientific foundations. In fact it is you
who claim to be proceeding on the lines of empiricism towards laws of universal validity, while I
have been suggesting that these and other scientific
terms which you are fond of using have no real
meaning in a historical argument. Even just now,
didn't you deduce from the conquest of the mystery

of the atom the certainty that man's mind will be able to conquer the mystery of the historical process as well? In my opinion these are fundamentally different propositions.

Let me remind you especially of what I have been saying about the uncertain nature of historical events, and the difficulty of detaching them from their contexts. And also of my contention that the cases and instances strewn over your pages have been arbitrarily selected from an infinite number and haven't therefore that value as evidence which you attach to them.

Professor Toynbee

There can be no doubt that you look upon this last point as an important one. . . . I see what you're getting at. I set out to deal with history in terms of civilizations, of which there are, of course, very few specimens, but in the illustrations I give, and the points I make, I don't confine myself to these rare big fellows, I hop about all over the place, bringing up as illustrations of my points events on a much smaller scale, which to you seem to be chosen arbitrarily, because they're just a few taken out of a large number. They also, as you point out, lend themselves to more interpretations than one. Yes, I think that's fair criticism, and quite telling. In answer I'd say two things. I think, as I said a minute or two ago, the same historical event often can be analyzed legitimately in a number of different ways, each of which brings out some aspect of historical truth which is true as far as it goes, though not the whole truth. I have myself sometimes made the same historical event do double or treble duty in this way, and I don't think this is a misleading way of using facts. As I've said before, several different dissections can all be correct, each in its own line.

My second point is that I bring in these illustrations taken from the small change of history, not for their own sake but to throw indirect light on the big units, which I call civilizations, which are my main concern. I helped myself out in this way because, in the very early stage in human history in which our generation happens to be living, the number of civilizations that have come into existence up to date, is still so small—not more than about twenty, as I make it out.

To take up the case of your own country, Holland, now, which I have used to throw light on the rise of the Egyptian and Sumerian civilizations: you challenged my account of Holland's rise to greatness. I found my explanation of it in the stimulus of a hard country. The people of Holland had to wrest the country from the sea and they rose to the occasion.

Your criticism is that I've arbitrarily isolated one fact out of several. The Dutch, you say, didn't do it by themselves, they were helped at the start by efficient outsiders, and then the country, when it had been reclaimed, turned out to have a rich soil, as well as a good situation for commerce.

Yes, of course, those are also facts of Dutch history, but my answer is that they're not the key facts. If the outsiders that you have in mind are the Romans, well, the benefits of Roman efficiency were not enjoyed by Holland alone; Belgium, France and England enjoyed them as well. So Holland's Roman apprenticeship won't account for achievements that are special to Holland and that distinguish her from her neighbors. Then the fertile soil and good location: these aren't causes of Holland's great feat of fighting and beating the North Sea, they're effects and rewards of it. It is a case of "to him that hath, shall be given." What the Dutch had, before these other things were given them, was the strength of will to raise their country out of the waters. The terrific challenge of the sea to a country below sea level is surely the unique and distinguishing feature of Dutch history. With all deference to you, Geyl, as a Netherlander and a historian, I still think I'm right in picking out the response of the people of Holland to this challenge as being the key to the greatness of your country. I do also think that the case of Holland throws valuable light on the cases of Egypt and Babylonia, two other places where people have had to fight swamp and sea in order to reclaim land, and where this struggle between man and nature has brought to life two out of the twenty or so civilizations known to us.

Of course if one could lay hands on some more civilizations, one might be able to study history on that scale without having to bother about little bits and pieces like Holland and England. I wish I were in that happy position, and if you now, Geyl, would help me by taking up your archeological spade and unearthing a few more forgotten civilizations for me, I should be vastly obliged to you. But even if you proved yourself a Layard, Schliemann and Arthur Evans rolled into one, you could only raise my present figure of twenty-one known civilizations to twenty-four, and that of course wouldn't help me to reduce my margin of error appreciably.

To turn for a moment to a different point, I want to correct an impression that I think our listeners may have got, of something else that you were saying just now. Anyway, I got the impression myself that you still thought I claimed to be able to foretell the future from the past, that I'd laid it down that our own civilization was doomed. This is a very important point and I want to make my position on it clear beyond all possibility of mistake. So let me repeat: I don't set up to be a prophet, I don't believe history can be used for telling the world's fortune, I think history can perhaps sometimes show one possibilities or even probabilities, but never certainties. With the awful warning of Spengler's dogmatic determinism before my eyes, I always have been and shall be mighty careful, for my part, to treat the future of our own civilization as an open question— not at all because I'm afraid of committing myself, but because I believe as strongly as you do, Geyl, that it *is* an open question.

Professor Geyl

Well I'm glad, Toynbee, that you've taken so seriously the objections I've made to the profusion of illustrations from national histories. As to the case of Holland, let me just say that I was not thinking of the Romans only and not even of foreigners primarily. What I meant was that Netherlands civilization did not have its origin or earliest development in the region which was exposed to the struggle with the water, but, on the contrary, this region could be described as a backward part of the Netherlands area as a whole. And as regards the future, in one place of your book you are very near to drawing—

as you put it—"the horoscope of our civilization" from the fates of other civilizations, and you suggest repeatedly that we have got into the disintegration stage, which you picture to us so elaborately in your book as leading inevitably to catastrophe. I'm glad to hear now that you did not in fact mean to pass an absolute sentence of death over us.

PROFESSOR TOYNBEE

No, I think we simply don't know. I suppose I must be the last judge of what my own beliefs are.

But now, Geyl, here is a ball I'd like for a change to bowl at you. You've given me an opening by the fair-mindedness and frankness you've shown all through our debate. You've done justice to my contention that while historical facts are in some respects unique, there are other respects in which they belong to a class and are therefore comparable. There is truth, you say, in this, otherwise no general ideas about history could ever be formed, but isolating the comparable elements is ticklish work. It certainly is ticklish work. I speak with feeling from long experience in trying to do precisely that job. But may there not be a moral in this for you and every other historian as well as for me? May not it mean that we ought all of us to give far more time and far more serious and strenuous thought than many of us have ever given to this job of forming one's general ideas? And there is a previous and, to my mind, more important job to be done before that.

We've first to bring into consciousness our existing ideas and to put these trump cards of ours face upwards on the table. All historians are bound, you see, to have general ideas about history. On this point, every stitch of work they do is so much evidence against them. Without ideas, they couldn't think a thought, speak a sentence or write a line on their subjects. Ideas are the machine tools of the mind, and, wherever you see a thought being thrown out, you may be certain that there is an idea at the back of it. This is so obvious that I find it hard to have patience with historians who boast, as some modern Western historians do, that they keep entirely to the facts of history and don't go in for theories. Why, every so-called fact that they present to you had some pattern of theory behind it. Historians who genuinely believe they have no general ideas about history are, I would suggest to them, simply ignorant of the workings of their own minds, and such wilful ignorance is, isn't it, really unpardonable. The intellectual worker who refuses to let himself become aware of the working ideas with which he is operating seems to me to be about as great a criminal as the motorist who first closes his eyes and then steps on the gas. To leave oneself and one's public at the mercy of any fool ideas, if they happen to have taken possession of one's unconscious, is surely the height of intellectual irresponsibility.

I believe our listeners would be very much interested to hear what you say about that

PROFESSOR GEYL

This is very simple. I agree with you entirely about the impossibility of allowing, as it used to be put, the facts to speak for themselves, and the historian who imagines that he can rule out theory or, let us say, his own individual mind, his personal view of things in general, seems to me a very uninteresting being, or in the majority of cases, when he is obviously only deluding himself and covering his particular partiality with the great word of objectivity and historical science, a very naïve person, and perhaps a very dangerous one.

As a matter of fact this is the spirit in which I have tackled you. When you said that I was an adherent of the nonsense view of history, you were mistaking my position altogether. In my own fashion, when I reject your methods and your conclusions, I am also trying to establish general views about history. Without such views, I know that the records of the past would become utterly chaotic and senseless, and I think I should rather be an astronomer than devote my life to so hopeless and futile a study.

But, to me, one of the great things to realize about history is its infinite complexity, and, when I say infinite, I do mean that not only the number of the phenomena and incidents but their often shadowy and changing nature is such that the attempt to reduce them to a fixed relationship and to a scheme of absolute validity can never lead to anything but disappointment. It is when you present your system in so hard and fast a manner as to seem, at any rate to me, to dictate to the future, that I feel bound to protest, on behalf both of history and of the civilization whose crisis we are both witnessing.

You have twitted me for inviting the world to sail on an uncharted course. Yet I believe that the sense of history is absolutely indispensable for the life of mankind. I believe with Burckhardt that there is wisdom to be gained from the study of the past, but no definite lessons for the actual problems of the present.

PROFESSOR TOYNBEE

Well there! It looks as if, on this question anyway, our two different approaches have brought us on to something like common ground. If I am right in this,

I think it is rather encouraging, for this last issue we were discussing is, I am sure, a fundamental one.

PROFESSOR GEYL

Well I see, Toynbee, that our time is up. There are just a few seconds left for me to pay tribute to the courage with which you, as you expressed it yourself, have risked your neck; not by facing me here at the microphone, but by composing that gigantic and impressive scheme of civilizations, which was bound to rouse the skeptics and to be subjected to their criticism. Now I am not such a skeptic as to doubt the rightness of my own position in our debate, but I am one compared with you. Perhaps you will value the assurance from such a one that he himself has found your great work immensely stimulating and that, generally speaking, in the vast enterprise in which we historians are engaged together, daring and imaginative spirits like yourself have an essential function to fulfil.

Toynbee's Philosophy of History

By PITIRIM A. SOROKIN

I. OUTLINE AND APPRECIATION

REGARDLESS OF THE SUBSEQUENT CRITICISM, Arnold J. Toynbee's *A Study of History* [1] is one of the most significant works of our time in the field of historical synthesis. Although several volumes of it are yet to come, six published volumes display a rare combination of the thoughtfulness of a philosopher with the technical competence of a meticulous empiricist. The combination insures against the sterile scholarship of a thoughtless "fact-finder," as well as against a fantastic flight of an incompetent dilettante. Hence its significance for historians, philosophers of history, sociologists, political scientists, and for anyone who is interested in the how and why of emergence, growth, decline, and dissolution of civilizations.

Mr. Toynbee starts with a thesis that the proper field of historical study is neither a description of

[1] *A Study of History.* By Arnold J. Toynbee. 6 volumes. Oxford University Press, 1934–39.

singularistic happenings contiguous in space or time, nor a history of the states and bodies politic or of mankind as a "unity."

The "intelligible fields of historical study" . . . are societies which have a greater extension, in both Space and Time, than national states or city-states, or any other political communities. . . . Societies, not states, are "the social atoms" with which students of history have to deal [I, 45].

Combining religious characteristics and territorial and partly political characteristics, he takes "civilization" as the proper object of historical study, in which "civilization" is "a species of society" (I, 129ff.). Of such civilizations, he takes twenty-one (later twenty-six) "related and unrelated" species: the Western, two Orthodox Christian (in Russia and the Near East), the Iranic, the Arabic, the Hindu, two Far Eastern, the Hellenic, the Syriac, the Indic, the Sinic, the Minoan, the Sumeric, the Hittite, the Babylonic, the Andean, the Mexic, the Yucatec, the Mayan, the Egyptiac, plus five "arrested civilizations": Polynesian, Eskimo, Nomadic, Ottoman, and Spartan (I, 132ff.; IV, 1ff.). With these twenty-six civilizations at his disposal, Toynbee attacks, first, the problem of genesis of civilization: Why do some of the societies, like many primitive groups, become static at an early stage of their existence and not emerge as civilizations while other societies reach this level?

His answer is that the genesis of civilization is due neither to the race factor nor to geographic environment as such but to a specific combination of two conditions: the presence of a creative minority in a given society and of an environment which is neither too unfavorable nor too favorable. The groups which had these conditions emerged as civilizations; the groups which did not have them remained on the subcivilization level. The mechanism of the birth of civilization in these conditions is formulated as an interplay of Challenge-and-Response. The environment of the above type incessantly challenges the society; and the society, through its creative minority, successfully responds to the challenge and solves the need. A new challenge follows, and a new response successfully ensues; and so the process goes on incessantly. In these conditions no possibility of rest exists, the society is on the move all the time, and such a move brings it, sooner or later, to the stage of civilization. Surveying the conditions in which his twenty-one civilizations were born, he finds that they emerged exactly in the above circumstances (I, 188–338; Vol. II, *passim*).

The next problem of the study is why and how, out of twenty-six civilizations, four (Far Western Christian, Far Eastern Christian, Scandinavian, and

Syriac) miscarried and turned out to be abortive; five (Polynesian, Eskimo, Nomadic, Spartan, and Ottoman) were arrested in their growth at an early stage; while the remaining civilizations grew "through an *élan* that carried them from challenge through response to further challenge and from differentiation through integration to differentiation again?" (III, 128).

The answer evidently depends upon the meaning of growth and its symptoms. In Toynbee's opinion the growth of civilization is not a geographic expansion of the society and is not due to it. If anything, the geographic expansion of a society is positively associated with retardation and disintegration but not with the growth (III, 128ff.). Likewise, the growth of civilization does not consist in, and is not due to, technological progress and the society's increasing mastery over the physical environment: ". . . there is no correlation between progress in technique and progress in civilization" (III, 173–74). The growth of civilization consists in "a progressive and cumulative inward self-determination or self-articulation" of the civilization; in a progressive and cumulative "etherialization" of the society's values and "simplification of the civilization's apparatus and technique" (III, 128ff., 182ff.). Viewed in the aspect of the intrasocial and inter-individual relationship, growth is an incessant creative "withdrawal and return" of the charismatic minority of the society in the process of the ever new successful responses to ever new challenges of the environment (III, 248ff.). Growing civilization is a unity. Its society consists of the creative minority freely imitated and followed by the majority—the Internal Proletariat of the society and the External Proletariat of its barbarian neighbors. In such a society there is no fratricidal struggle, no hard and fast divisions. It is a solidary body. Growing civilization unfolds its dominant potentialities, which are different in different civilizations: aesthetic in the Hellenic civilization; religious in the Indic and Hindu; scientifically machinistic in the Western; and so on (III, 128–390). As a result, the process of growth represents a progressive integration and self-determination of the growing civilization and a differentiation between the different civilizations in growth. Such is the solution of the problem of growth of civilization.

The third main problem of the study is how and why civilizations break down, disintegrate, and dissolve. They evidently do so because, out of twenty-six species of civilizations, "only four have miscarried as against twenty-six that have been born alive," and "no less than sixteen out of these twenty-six are by now dead and buried" (the Egyptiac, the Andean, the Sinic, the Minoan, the Sumeric, the Mayan, the Indic, the Hittite, the Syriac, the Hellenic, the Babylonic, the Mexic, the Arabic, the Yucatec, the Spartan, and the Ottoman). Of the remaining ten civilizations living,

the Polynesian and the Nomadic civilizations are now in their last agonies and seven out of eight others are all, in different degrees, under threat of either annihilation or assimilation by our own civilization of the West. Moreover, no less than six out of these seven civilizations . . . bear marks of having broken down and gone into disintegration [IV, 1–2].

Toynbee points out that the decline is not due to some cosmic necessity or to geographic factors or to racial degeneration or to external assaults of the enemies, which, as a rule, reinforce the growing civilization; neither is it caused by the decline of technique and technology, because "it is always the decline of civilization that is the cause and the decline of technique the consequence or symptom" (IV, 40).

The main difference between the process of growth and disintegration is that in the growth phase the civilization successfully responds to a series of ever new challenges, while in the disintegration stage it fails to give such a response to a given challenge. It tries to answer it again and again, but recurrently fails. In growth the challenges, as well as responses, vary all the time; in disintegration, the responses vary, but the challenge remains unanswered and unremoved. The author's verdict is that civilizations perish through suicide but not by murder (IV, 120). In Toynbee's formulation

the nature of the breakdowns of civilizations can be summed up in three points: a failure of creative power in the minority, an answering withdrawal of mimesis on the part of the majority, and a consequent loss of social unity in the society as a whole.

In an unfolded form this formula runs as follows:

When in the history of any society a Creative Minority degenerates into a mere Dominant Minority which attempts to retain by force a position which it has ceased to merit, this fatal change in the character of the ruling element provokes, on the other hand, the secession of a Proletariat (the majority) which no longer spontaneously admires or freely imitates the ruling element, and which revolts against being reduced to the status of an unwilling "underdog." This Proletariat, when it asserts itself, is divided from the outset into two distinct parts. There is an "Internal Proletariat" (the majority of the members) and . . . an "External Proletariat" of barbarians beyond the pale who now violently resist incorporation. And thus the breakdown of a civilization gives rise to a class war within the body social of a society which was neither divided against itself by hard-and-fast divisions nor sundered from its neighbors by unbridgeable gulfs so long as it was in growth [IV, 6].

This declining phase consists of three subphases: (*a*) breakdown of the civilization, (*b*) its disintegration, and (*c*) its dissolution. The breakdown and dissolution are often separated by centuries, even thousands of years, from one another. For instance, the breakdown of the Egyptiac civilization occurred in the sixteenth century B.C., and its dissolution only in the fifth century A.D. For two thousand years between breakdown and dissolution it existed in a "petrified life-in-death." In a similar "petrified" state up to the present time the Far Eastern civilization continues in China after its breakdown in the ninth century A.D. About one thousand and eight hundred years, respectively, elapsed between these points in the history of the Sumeric and Hellenic civilizations (IV, 62ff.; V, 2ff.); and so on. Like a petrified tree trunk, such a society can linger in that stage of life-in-death for centuries, even thousands of years. Nevertheless, the destiny of most, if not of all, civilizations, seems to be to come to final dissolution sooner or later. As to the Western society, though it seems to have had all the symptoms of breakdown and disintegration, the author is noncommittal. He still leaves a hope for a miracle: "We may and must pray that a reprieve which God has granted to our society once will not be refused if we ask for it again in a contrite spirit and with a broken heart" (VI, 321).

Such being the general nature of the decline of civilizations, a most detailed analysis of its uniformities, symptoms, and phases is developed in Volumes IV, V, and VI. Only a few of these uniformities can be touched on here. While in the growth period the Creative Minority gives a series of successful responses to ever new challenges, now, in the disintegration period, it fails to do so. Instead, intoxicated by victory, it begins to "rest on one's oars," to "idolize" the relative values as absolute; loses its charismatic attraction and is not imitated and followed by the majority. Therefore, more and more it has now to use force to control the Internal and the External Proletariat. In this process it creates a "Universal State," like the Roman Empire created by the Hellenic Dominant Minority, as a means to keep itself and the civilization alive; enters into wars; becomes slave of the intractable institutions; and works its own and its civilization's ruin.

The "Internal Proletariat" now secedes from the Minority; becomes dissatisfied and disgruntled; and often creates a "Universal Church"—for instance, Christianity or Buddhism—as its own creed and institution. While the "Universal State" of the Dominant Minority is doomed, the Universal Church of the Inner Proletariat (for instance, Christianity) serves as a bridge and foundation for a new civilization, "apparented" by, and affiliated with, the old one.

The External Proletariat now organizes itself and begins to attack the declining civilization, instead of striving to be incorporated by it. In this way the Schism enters the Body and Soul of civilization. It results in an increase of strife and fratricidal wars that work in favor of the development of the ruin. The Schism in the Soul manifests itself in the profound change of the mentality and behavior of the members of the disintegrating society. It leads to an emergence of four types of personality and "Saviors": Archaist, Futurist (Saviors by Sword), Detached and Indifferent Stoic, and finally, Transfigured Religious Savior, posited in the supersensory world of God. The sense of Drift, of Sin, begins to grow; Promiscuity and Syncretism become dominant. Vulgarization and "Proletarization" invade arts and sciences, philosophy and language, religion and ethics, manners and institutions.

But all in vain. With the exception of Transfiguration, all these efforts and "Saviors" do not stop the disintegration. At best the civilization can become "Fossilized"; and in this form, "life-in-death" can linger for centuries and even thousands of years; but its dissolution, as a rule, comes. The only fruitful way turns out to be the way of Transfiguration, the transfer of the goal and values to the supersensory Kingdom of God. It may not stop the disintegration of the given civilization, but it may serve as a seed for emergence and development of a new affiliated civilization; and through that, it is a step forward to the eternal process of elevation of Man to Superman, of "the City of Man to City of God," as the ultimate terminal point of Man and Civilization. The volumes close with an almost apocalyptic note:

The aim of Transfiguration is to give light to them that sit in darkness . . . it is pursued by seeking the Kingdom of God in order to bring its life . . . into action. . . . The goal of Transfiguration is thus the Kingdom of God [VI, 171].

The whole human history or the total civilizational process thus turns into a Creative Theodicy; through separate civilizations and their uniform, but concretely different, rhythms, the reality unfolds its richness and leads from "under-Man" and "under-Civilization," to Man and Civilization, and finally to Superman and Transfigured Etherial Super-Civilization of the Kingdom of God.

The work of the Spirit of the Earth, as he waves and draws his threads on the Loom of Time, is the temporal history of Man as this manifests itself in the geneses and growths and breakdowns and disintegrations of human societies; and in all this welter of life . . . we can hear the beat of an elemental rhythm . . . of Challenge-and-Response and Withdrawal-and-Return and Rout-and-

Rally and Apparentation-and-Affiliation and Schism-and-Palingenesia. This elemental rhythm is the alternating beat of Yin and Yang. . . . The Perpetual turning of a wheel is not a vain repetition if, at each revolution, it is carrying a vehicle that much nearer to its goal; and if "palingenesia" signifies the birth of something new . . . then the Wheel of Existence is not just a devilish device for inflicting an everlasting torment on a damned Ixion. The music that the rhythm of Yin and Yang beats out is the song of creation. . . . Creation would not be creative if it did not swallow up in itself all things in Heaven and Earth, including its own antithesis [VI, 324].

Such is the general skeleton of Toynbee's philosophy of history. It is clothed by him in a rich and full-blooded body of facts, empirical verification, and a large number of subpropositions. The main theses, as well as the subpropositions, are painstakingly tested by the known empirical facts of the history of the twenty-one civilizations studied. In this respect the theory of Toynbee, conceived and executed on a grand plan, is probably documented more fully than most of the existing philosophies of history. To repeat, the work as a whole is a real contribution to the field of historical synthesis.

II. CRITICISM

IF WE NOW ASK HOW VALID is the general scheme of Toynbee's theory of the rise and decline of civilizations as well as a number of his secondary propositions, the situation changes. Side by side with the unquestionable virtues, the work has very serious shortcomings. Among the unessential and superfluous defects, the following can be mentioned: First, the work is too voluminous and could have been compressed without losing anything in the clearness and completeness of its theory. A pronounced penchant of the author to quote abundantly from the Bible, mythology, poetry—to use overabundant poetic and symbolic images—is partly responsible for this insignificant defect.

Second, in spite of an astounding erudition, the author displays either an ignorance or a deliberate neglect of many important sociological works, which deal more fundamentally with the problems Toynbee is struggling with than other works quoted. Neither the names of Tarde, Durkheim, Max Weber, Pareto, nor those of practically any sociologist are mentioned. One of the consequences of such a neglect is that Toynbee has to write dozens and hundreds of pages on questions that were studied in such works more thoroughly and better than Toynbee does. For instance, mimesis or imitation is one of the cardinal points of his theory to which he devotes many pages. A reader who knows Tarde's *Laws of Imitation,* not to mention many later works, does not get from Toynbee's analysis anything new. More than that: Toynbee's theory of mimesis and of its uniformities has many mistakes which would have been avoided if he had studied some of the main works in this field. Similarly, he devotes several hundreds of pages—in Volumes I and II—to investigation of the influence of race and geographic environment upon societies and civilization. And yet, he does not add anything new to the existing knowledge in that field. Even more, he fails to see the demonstrated weaknesses of the claims of some of the climatic and racial theories (like that of Huntington) which he accepts to a considerable extent. A concise characterization of the existing conclusions in these fields would have permitted him to outline his theory on only a few pages and to avoid several pitfalls into which he has fallen. The same criticism can be applied to several other problems. In spite of the extraordinary erudition of the author, it shows itself somewhat one-sided and inadequate.

Third, his knowledge of the history of the twenty-six civilizations he deals with is very uneven. It is excellent in the field of the Hellenic (Greco-Roman) civilization, and it is much thinner in the field of other civilizations.

Fourth, his acquaintance with the extant knowledge in the field of such phenomena as art, philosophy, science, law, and some others with which he deals, seems also to be inadequate: little, if anything.

is quoted in these fields, and the conclusions of the author sound superficial and dilettante.

Fifth, the same is true of several other fields in which he makes categorical statements. For instance, he contends that "the evil of War in the eighteenth century [was reduced] to a minimum which has never been approached in . . . our Western history, either before or after, up to date" (IV, 143). As a matter of fact, our systematic study of the movement of war (see my *Social and Cultural Dynamics*, Vol. III) shows that, measured either by the number of war casualties or by the size of the armies per million of population, the centuries from twelve to sixteen, inclusive, and the nineteenth century were less belligerent than the eighteenth century. In Volume V, page 43, he himself seems to repudiate his previous statement by saying that "the life of our Western Society has been as grievously infested by the plague of war during the last four centuries as in any earlier age." As a further example: he contends that "the sense of drift" as manifested in various deterministic philosophies grows with the process of disintegration in all civilizations (V, 422ff.). The factual movement of deterministic conceptions versus indeterministic is very different from what he claims it is (see my *Dynamics*, Vol. II, chap. ix). A third example: he contends that in a diffusion or radiation of a given culture the alien culture is penetrated first by the economic elements; second, by the political; and third, by the cultural elements. In this way a uniformity of the order of the penetration of the alien culture by specified elements of diffusing civilization is set forth (IV, 57). As a matter of fact, such uniformity does not exist. In some cases the economic elements penetrate first; in others, the cultural (see the evidences in Vol. IV of my *Dynamics*).

In the work there are many similar blunders and overstatements. However, in a work of such immense magnitude as *A Study of History* such shortcomings are inevitable. One should not carp at them. If the main conceptual scheme of the author is solid, such shortcomings can easily be discounted as superfluous.

Unfortunately, the work has two fundamental defects, which concern not the details but the heart and soul of Toynbee's philosophy of history. They concern, first, *"the civilization" taken by Toynbee as a unit of historical study; second, the conceptual scheme of genesis, growth, and decline of the civilizations put at the foundation of Toynbee's philosophy of history*. Let us look at these assumptions more closely.

By "civilization" Toynbee means not a mere "field of historical study" but a united system, or the whole, whose parts are connected with one another by causal ties. Therefore, as in any causal system in his "civilization," parts must depend upon one another, upon the whole, and the whole upon its parts. He categorically states again and again that

civilizations are wholes whose parts all cohere with one another and all affect one another reciprocally. . . . It is one of the characteristics of civilizations in process of growth that all aspects and activities of their social life are coordinated into a single social whole, in which the economic, political, and cultural elements are kept in a nice adjustment with one another by an inner harmony of the growing body social [III, 380, 152; see also I, 34ff., 43ff., 149ff., 153ff.].

Thus, like so-called "functional anthropologists," he assumes that his "civilizations" are a real system and not mere congeries or conglomerations of various cultural (or civilizational) phenomena and objects adjacent in space or time but devoid of any causal or meaningful ties (see the analysis of socio-cultural systems and congeries in my *Social and Cultural Dynamics*, Vol. I, chap. i; an unfolded theory of socio-cultural systems is given in Vol. IV of the *Dynamics*). If civilizations are real systems, then, as in any causal system, we should expect that when one important component of it changes, the rest of the components change too, because if A and B are causally connected, then the change of A is followed by the change of B in a definite and uniform manner. Otherwise, A and B are mere congeries but not the partners of the causal system. Is Toynbee's assumption valid? I am afraid it is not: his *"civilizations" are not united systems but mere conglomerations of various civilizational objects and phenomena* (congeries of systems and singular cultural traits) *united only by special adjacency but not by causal or meaningful bonds. For this reason, they are not real "species of society"; therefore they can hardly be treated as unities and can hardly have any uniformities in their genesis, growth, and decline.* These concepts cannot even be applied to the congeries, because congeries do not and cannot grow or decline. Like the components of a dumping place, they can only be rearranged, added to, or subtracted from; but we cannot talk of the growth or decline of a "civilizational dumping place" or of any merely spatial conglomeration of things and events. This diagnosis of the "civilizations" is inadvertently corroborated many times by Toynbee himself. In many places of his work he indicates that, for instance, the technique and economic life of the civilization often change while the rest of the civilization does not change; in other cases the rest of the civilization changes while technique remains static; in still other cases, the technique changes in one way while the rest of the civilization moves in the opposite direction (IV, 40ff.; III, 154ff., *et passim*). If we have A and B where the change of one of the variables is not followed by that of the other, or when it does not show any uniform variation, this means A and B are causally unrelated; therefore they are not components of the same system or parts of the same whole. Toynbee himself demonstrates—and demonstrates well—that two of the components of his civilization (technique and economy) are causally unrelated to the rest of the "whole." His whole—"civilization"—thus turns out into a mere spatial congeries. In other places of his work he gives several cases where the religious or the artistic or the political element of his whole—civilization—each appears to be an independent variable unrelated to the rest of the alleged "whole." In this way Toynbee himself repudiates his basic assumption that his "civilizations" are "the wholes whose parts all cohere together."

In fact, it is easy to show—and show convincingly—that any of his civilizations is not a "whole" or a system at all but a mere coexistence of an enormous number of systems and congeries existing side by side and not united either by causal or meaningful or any other ties (necessary for any real system) except a mere contiguity in space and time. Such a contiguity or mere spatial adjacency does not make from "a book + worn out shoes + bottle of whiskey" lying side by side any unity, whole, or system. It remains a congeries. Not only is the total civilization of such enormous "culture-areas" as the Greco-Roman, or the Sinic, or of any other of his civilizations not one whole or system, but the total civilization of even a smallest possible civilizational area—that of a single individual—is but a coexistence of several and different systems and congeries unrelated with one another in any way except spatial adjacency in a biological organism. Suppose that an individual is a Roman Catholic, Republican, professor, preferring Romantic music to Classic, Scotch to rye, blondes to brunettes. Roman Catholicism does not require, causally or logically, the Republican instead of the Democratic or other party; the Republican party is not connected logically or causally with professorial occupation. This is true also with a preference for Scotch to rye, or Romantic music to the Classic. We have Roman Catholics who are not Republicans, and Republicans who are not Roman Catholics, professors who are neither, and many in other occupations who are Catholics or Republicans. Some Catholics or Republicans or professors prefer Scotch to rye, some rye to Scotch, some do not drink whiskey, some prefer beer to wine, and so on. This means that the total "civilization" of the same individual is not one unified system but a conglomeration of various systems and singular "civ-

ilizational" traits united only by a spatial adjacency of
the same biological organism. A biological organism,
being a real system, changes biologically as a whole;
but its total "civilization," being congeries, does not
change in togetherness, nor can the "total civilizations" of many individuals display any uniformity in
their change. (See my *Dynamics*, Vol. I, chap. i; and
Vol. IV, for a systematic analysis of this problem.)

If, then, the total "civilization" of an individual is
not one system, still less is one system the total civilization of a city block, or of the total city, of a nation,
and of the still larger "civilized societies" of Toynbee.
This means that Toynbee's "civilization" is not "species" but a kind of a "large dumping place" where
coexist, side by side, an enormous number of various
sociocultural systems many of which are not related
to one another either causally or meaningfully: the
State system, the Religious systems, the Art-Ethics-
Philosophy-Science-Economic-Political-Technologi-
cal and other systems and congeries "dumped together" over a vast territory and carried on by a multitude of individuals. One cannot style as species of
the same genus different sets of incidental congeries: "shoe-watch-bottle-*Saturday Evening Post*"
here, "trousers-comb-detective story-valve-rose-auto-
mobile" there: and still less can one expect uniformities of structure and change in genesis, growth, and

decline of such different congeries. Having mistakenly taken different congeries for system, Toynbee begins to treat his civilizations as "species of society" and valiantly hunts for uniformities in their genesis, growth, and decline. In this way he makes the fatal mistake of erecting an enormous building upon a foundation less stable than the proverbial sand.

All the subsequent defects of his theory follow from this "original sin." It is aggravated by another fatal mistake he commits, namely, by the acceptance of the old—from Florus to Spengler—conceptual scheme of "genesis-growth-decline," as a uniform pattern of change of civilizations. Such a conception is possibly the worst among all the existing schemes of change of civilizations; and it is doubly fatal for Toynbee's theory. Indeed, if his civilizations are mere congeries, for this reason only we cannot talk of the genesis, growth, breakdown, disintegration, and dissolution of congeries. Congeries are neither born (alive or abortively) nor can they grow or disintegrate, since they never have been integrated. Generally, this popular conceptual scheme is purely analogical and represents not a theory of how sociocultural phenomena change but an evaluative theory of sociocultural progress: how they *should* change. Therefore, Toynbee's theory is not so much a theory of civilizational change as much as an evaluative theory of civilizational progress or regress. This clearly comes out already in his formula of "growth" and "disintegration." They are evaluative formulas of progress and regress but not the formulas of change.

From these two sins follow all the factual and logical incongruities of Toynbee's philosophy of history. First, his classifications of civilizations. Many a historian, anthropologist, and sociologist will certainly object to it as arbitrary, having no clear logical *fundamentum divisionis*. Several Christian civilizations are treated as separate and different; while a conglomeration of different (religious and other) systems are united into one civilization. Sparta is arbitrarily cut out of the rest of the Hellenic civilization, while Roman civilization is made inseparable from the Greek or Hellenic. Polynesian and Eskimo civilizations or "under-civilizations" (in one part Toynbee states that they were live-born civilizations; in another he claims that they remained at "sub-civilizational" level and have never reached the state of civilizations)—each is taken as a separate civilization; while all the Nomads of all the continents are united into one civilization, and so on.

Second, Toynbee's mass onslaught against civilizations in making most of them either "abortively born," "arrested," or "petrified," or "broken-down" or "disintegrating" or "dead and buried." According to Toynbee, out of twenty-six civilizations, only one—the Western—is still possibly alive at the present time, all the others being either dead or half-dead ("arrested," "petrified," "disintegrating"). Since, according to the assumed scheme, civilizations must have breakdowns, disintegration, and death, the author must either bury them or make them "abortive," "arrested," "petrified," or at least broken down and disintegrating. Since such is the demand of the scheme and since Toynbee does not have any clear criteria as to what death or breakdown or integration or disintegration of civilization really is, he willingly takes the role of an undertaker of civilizations.

Third, courageously following his scheme, he is not deterred by the fact that some of his civilizations which, according to his scheme, ought to have been dead a long time ago, after their breakdown, lived centuries, even thousands of years, and are still alive and very much so. He disposes of the difficulty by a simple device of "petrified" civilizations. So China has been petrified for thousands of years; Egypt for some two thousands of years; so the Hellenic civilization was either disintegrating or petrified after the Peloponnesian War up to the fifth century A.D. The whole Roman history was but an incessant disintegration, from the very beginning to the end; and so other civilizations. In his scheme civilizations hardly have time to live and to grow; if they are not born abortive —as some are—they are arrested; if they are not arrested, they have their breakdown almost immediately after they are born and then begin to disintegrate or are turned into a "petrified trunk." Of course, philosophically the birth is the beginning of death; but an empirical investigator of either the life of an organism or of civilization can and must be less philosophical and can and must study the process of life itself, before the real death, or paralysis, or incurable sickness occurs. And for most of the organisms and civilizations there is a great distance between the terminal points of birth and death.

This means that Toynbee studies little the greater part of the existence of the civilizations and drowns centuries and thousands of years of their existence, activity, and change in his penchant of an "undertaker of civilizations." By this I do not deny the facts of either disintegration or even dissolution of real cultural or civilizational systems. Such facts occur, but occur with real systems, not with congeries of civilizations; and occur not immediately after the "birth" of the system but often after their long—sometimes indefinitely long—life and change. As a matter of fact, the elements of the congeries of Toynbee's civilizations still exist, even of those which he considers dead and buried a long time ago. Quite a large number of Egyptiac or Babylonic or especially Hellenic cultural systems and cultural traits (philosophy, ethics, architecture, sculpture, literature, art, and so on) are very much alive as components of the contemporary Western or other cultures. And they are alive not as objects of a museum but as living realities in our and other cultures.

Fourth, the foregoing explains why in Toynbee's work there is little of the analysis of the phase of the growth of the civilizations. There are only fairly indefinite statements that in that phase there is a Creative Minority successfully meeting the challenge, that there is no class war, no intersociety war, and that everything goes well there and everything moves and becomes more and more "etherialized." That is about all that is said of this phase. Such a characterization of the process of growth of his twenty-one civilizations is evidently fantastic in its "idyllic" and other virtues. If we have to believe it, we seemingly have to accept that in Greece before 431–403 B.C. (the breakdown of the Hellenic civilization, according to Toynbee) there were no wars, no revolutions, no class struggle, no slavery, no traditionalism, no uncreative minority, and that all these "plagues" appeared only after the Peloponnesian War. On the other hand, we expect to find that, after it, in Greece and Rome creativeness ceased, and that there was no Plato, no Aristotle, no Epicurus, no Zeno, no Polybius, no Church Fathers, no Lucretius, no scientific discovery—nothing creative. As a matter of fact, the factual situation in all these respects was very different before and after the breakdown. The indicators of war per million of the population for Greece were twenty-nine for the fifth, forty-eight for the fourth, and eighteen and three, respectively, for the third and second centuries B.C. Indicators of Internal Disturbances (revolutions) were 149, 468, 320, 259, and 36, respectively, for the centuries from the sixth to the second B.C., inclusive. This shows that the real movement of wars and revolutions in Greece was very different from what Toynbee tells us. The same is true of Rome (see the detailed data in my *Social and Cultural Dynamics*, Vol. III). The scientific, philosophical, and religious creativeness likewise reached their peak rather in and after the fifth century than before that time (see the figures of discoveries, inventions, and philosophical systems in *Dynamics*, Vol. II, chap. iii, *et passim*). In regard to the Western civilization, as mentioned, the diagnosis of Toynbee is somewhat ambiguous. In many places he says that it already had its breakdown and is in the process of disintegration; in other places he is noncommittal. Whatever is his diagnosis, the Western civilization before the fifteenth century is regarded by him in the phase of growth. If this is so, then, according to his scheme, no revolutions, no serious wars, no hard-and-fast class divisions must have existed in Europe before that century. Factually, the thirteenth and fourteenth centuries are the most revolutionary centuries up to the twentieth century in the history of Europe; likewise, serfdom and other class divisions were hard and fast, and there were many wars—small and great (see the data in Vols. II and III of my *Dynamics*). Finally, the medieval Western civilization of the period of growth does not exhibit many of the traits of Toynbee's growing civilizations but displays a mass of traits which are the characteristics of Toynbee's disintegrating civilizations. The same is true of his other civilizations. This means that Toynbee's uniformities of growth and decline of the civilizations are largely fantastic and are not borne out by the facts.

Fifth, a large number of the uniformities he claims in connection with his conceptual scheme are also either fallacious or overstated—for instance, his uniformity of negative correlation between the geographic expansion of civilization and its growth; between war and growth; between progress of technique and growth. Granting a part of truth to his statements, at the same time in this categoric formulation they are certainly fallacious. If Toynbee's twenty-one civilizations did not diffuse over large areas and a multitude of persons and remained just the civilization of a little Sumeric, Greek, Egyptiac, or Arabic village, they could hardly become "historical" and certainly would not come to the attention of historians and Toynbee and would not become one of his twenty-one civilizations. All his civilizations are vast complexes, spread over vast areas of territory and vast populations. They did not emerge at once in such a vast form; but in starting with a small area they expanded (in the process of their growth) over vaster and vaster areas and populations and through that became historical. Otherwise, they would not have been noticed. If Toynbee contends, as in a few places he does, that such a diffusion over vaster areas was performed peacefully, without war, through spontaneous submission of the "barbarians" to the charm of the diffusing civilization, such a statement is again inaccurate. All his twenty-one civilizations in their period of growth (according to Toynbee's scheme) expanded not only peacefully but with force, coercion, and wars. On the other hand, many of them in the period of disintegration shrank, rather than expanded, and were more peaceful than in the periods of Toynbee's growth.

Sixth, following Spengler, whose ghost heavily weighs upon the author, Toynbee ascribes different dominant tendencies to each of his civilizations: aesthetic to the Hellenic, religious to the Indic, machinistic-technological to the Western (he does not give further such dominant penchants to each of the remaining eighteen civilizations). Such a summary characterization is again very doubtful. The Western civilization did not show its alleged dominant characteristic at all up to approximately the thirteenth century A.D.: from the sixth to the end of the twelfth century the movement of technological inventions and scientific discoveries stood at about zero in this allegedly technological civilization par excellence; and from the sixth to the thirteenth century this machinistic civilization was religious through and through, even more religious than the Indic or Hindu civilizations in many periods of their history (see the data on discoveries and technological inventions in my *Dynamics,* Vol. II, chap. iii). The supposedly aesthetic Hellenistic civilization did not show its aesthetic penchant (in Toynbee's sense) before the sixth century B.C. and displayed quite a boisterous scientific and technological *élan* in the period from 600 to 200 A.D. (see the figures, Vol. II, chap. iii). The Arabic civilization (whose dominant trait Toynbee does not stress) displayed an enormous *élan* of scientific and technological penchant in the centuries from the eighth to the thirteenth—much more so than the Western civilization during these centuries (see the data, Vol. II, chap. iii). All this means that the Spenglerian-Toynbee ascription of some specific perennial tendency to this or that civilization, regardless of the period of its history, is misleading and inaccurate.

One can continue this criticism for a long time. A large part of the statements of Toynbee taken in his conceptual scheme are either inaccurate or invalid. However, many of these statements, properly reformulated and put in quite a different conceptual scheme of civilizational change, become valid and penetrating. For instance, most of the traits which Toynbee ascribes to the civilizations in their period of growth and partly in that of "petrification" are accurate for the phase of civilization dominated by what I call the "Ideational supersystem of culture" (not the total given culture in which it appears). Many of the characteristics of Toynbee's "disintegrating" period are typical for a phase of civilization dominated by what I call the "Sensate supersystem" (not the whole total culture or civilization). Many of the characteristics of Toynbee's stage of acute disorganization are but the characteristics of the period when a given culture passes from the domination of Ideational to Idealistic or Sensate supersystems, and vice versa. Such periods of shift happen several times in the history of this or that "total culture" or "civilization." They are, however, neither a death nor "petrification" nor "arrest" but merely a great transition from one supersystem to another. Put into this scheme, and reinterpreted, many pages and chapters of Toynbee's work become illuminating, penetrating, and scientifically valid. In such a setting his conception of the creative character of human history acquires still deeper meaning. Likewise, his hesitant diagnosis of the present state of the Western civilization becomes more definite and specific: as the status of the civilization entering not the path of death but the painful road of a great transition from the over-ripe Sensate phase to a more "etherialized" or spiritualized Ideational or Idealistic phase. Translated into more accurate terms of the real sociocultural systems and of the great rhythm of Sensate-Idealistic-Ideational supersystems of culture, *A Study of History* is a most stimulating and illuminating work of a distinguished thinker and scholar.

Publisher's Note

Toynbee's System of Civilizations, by Pieter Geyl, is reprinted from the *Journal of the History of Ideas,* January, 1948. The article is a translation by Dr. Geyl of his lecture delivered at Utrecht, Nov. 9, 1946, before the *Historisch Genootschap.*

The discussion between Pieter Geyl and Arnold J. Toynbee, *Can We Know the Pattern of the Past?,* was broadcast in the Third Programme of the British Broadcasting Corporation, London, on January 4 and March 7, 1948. It was published in book form by Uitgeverij F. G. Kroonder, Bussum, Holland, in 1948.

Toynbee's Philosophy of History, by Pitirim A. Sorokin, is reprinted from the *Journal of Modern History,* September, 1940.

Index